WISHBONE

WISHBONE

AN AMERICAN ODYSSEY IN ASIA

CAROL WRIGHT FOLBRE

FOREWORD BY NAOMI SHIHAB NYE

TRINITY UNIVERSITY PRESS
SAN ANTONIO, TEXAS

Trinity University Press
San Antonio, Texas 78212

Book design by Anne Boston
Author photo by Michael Taylor

ISBN 978-1-59534-281-2 hardcover
ISBN 978-1-59534-298-0 ebook

Trinity University Press strives to produce its books using methods and materials in an environmentally sensitive manner. We favor working with manufacturers that practice sustainable management of all natural resources, produce paper using recycled stock, and manage forests with the best possible practices for people, biodiversity, and sustainability. The press is a member of the Green Press Initiative, a nonprofit program dedicated to supporting publishers in their efforts to reduce their impacts on endangered forests, climate change, and forest-dependent communities. The paper used in this publication meets the minimum requirements of the American National Standard for Information Sciences—Permanence of Paper for Printed Library Materials, ansi 39.48–1992.

CIP data on file at the Library of Congress

29 28 27 26 25 | 5 4 3 2 1

To Lila and Callum—
Your GaGa and BaBa are young once
but always adventuresome

CONTENTS

FOREWORD

Naomi Shihab Nye

"I've always fed myself from this wishbone," writes Carol Folbre, as she invites us to her warm table of memory and magnificent wanderings.

Folbre writes and remembers with such tender elegance and detail; we are nourished in every fiber of our body and being. The concept of returning to one's own journals from some forty years before makes more sense than most things people do—to find how many early threads connect to now and how many images endure, and to contemplate how our youthful revelations unfolded.

In a time before internet and GPS, we found our ways. Folbre's book makes us wistful for a simpler, more tangible presence on this precious planet—deeper connections with one another, more trust, more faith, more confidence.

As lucky as my husband and I were to receive detailed, illustrated letters from Folbre's travels forty-plus years ago, I felt doubly lucky and kept getting younger and happier as I read her terrific book.

PREFACE

A memory at age six has never escaped me. What happened was supposed to be normal as I peeked my head over the kitchen counter. I blinked, then glanced away as my mother pursed her lips and ripped a thin, spur-shaped bone from a pink chicken breast. It wouldn't give easily; small pieces of flesh clung on for life. Then she seasoned and placed the bird in the oven, propped the bone on the windowsill to dry, and said, "We'll split that in a few days."

Ripping out a breastbone was brutal to me but matter-of-fact to my mother. Each day I watched the bone bleach and grow more sinewy, until my mother asked me to grab one end while she held the other. We tugged at the wishbone in opposite directions until it snapped. I got the end without the top knot. The short bone.

"The one with the long end gets good luck and marries first," Mother said, and smiled. "It's so random how life works." She left me in the kitchen with the short bone.

I felt abandoned, vulnerable, and maybe even taken advantage of by my own blood. In that moment I decided that even if I wasn't nurtured, I would nurture myself . . . others . . . and life.

Years later I understand the full meaning of that lesson. We're all made of long bones and short bones. It's random how circumstances seem to dole out what economic situations we are born in, our race, nationality, religion, spiritual life, mental or physical health. I've had both the long end and the short end of the stick. What I've chosen to do with this knowledge makes the difference. When I have the long end, I'm now conscious of whether I'm hoarding it, flaunting it, or desiring even in the smallest way to take advantage of the less fortunate. This change took me half a century.

What's the gain of personal wealth if it's at the expense of the most vulnerable? Where does satisfaction lie? Is there really any equity? I'm finally asking these questions because of traveling and living with those whose cultures don't match my own. Why, when, where, and how does life shift? Travel with me and see.

≡

A low ember burned within me at age twenty-five, then sputtered like a firecracker. Next on the agenda of an ordinary life—something I feared like eating Spam—would be the purchase of our own home and new cars, and having kids where I grew up, in Alamo Heights, a neighborhood in central Texas. I had been married for three years, with a perfect life. Most people called it nirvana, but something was missing.

I'd known security as a child only as restlessness, angst, and risk. I planned to be an artist and novelist and to look at life in a detached way, so I quit my job teaching English in a federal Title 1 program in Alamo Heights.

How could I teach kids who didn't have their basic needs met? Yes, this was true even in suburban Alamo Heights. They didn't feel safe, not even in a classroom. Why should they study grammar when they were fighting turf wars at home? I didn't have any understanding of worlds or cultures like theirs. I helplessly watched while gang leaders picked a fight in my classroom, disrupting my lesson on dependent clauses. In that moment, these students became independent clauses.

Wasn't there a bigger world than my San Antonio private club culture? Most people would die to be members of elite organizations like this so young in life. The beautiful world in my palm seemed like an illusion, a trap hidden beneath the Astroturf.

I yearned to travel the world to experience a global, cultural perspective. This was my wishbone. Then maybe I could teach and give with a seasoned mind.

My husband, Banks, composed himself and calmly asked why I wanted to travel rather than just go on vacation. He knew I had passions that could be fulfilled in unexpected, beautiful ways. We could have it all. But, practically, how was he supposed to juggle a Texas law practice while living on an island in Thailand?

The only experience I'd had living in another culture was in Brazil right out of college. I stayed with a college roommate's Brazilian parents, who were strict Christian Scientists living in the mountain shadow of the statue of Christ, Corcovado, in Rio de Janeiro.

This was the beginning of imbibing the spirit of other cultures. I wasn't conscious of this or the fact that I was on the cusp of letting my life fit into a bigger story.

I liked being an undocumented worker in Rio teaching English to Portuguese professionals for three months. I had a passport and visa but no green card. When I wasn't working, I traveled by bus through the crowded streets of Carnival or visited Copacabana and twelve other curvy beaches where the schools were located.

One day I panicked that something might be in the matte tea I drank, since the dogs, cats, fleas, and many teens all seemed to be pregnant. It turned out that the family had some kind of business finding abandoned babies and placing them in homes around the world. We drove to clinics in nearby favelas (propped up cardboard villages) and checked for unwanted newborns. Sometimes babies were placed on our doorstep, like the two the family was currently nursing back to health. I never asked questions, just observed, taught English as a foreign language, and quit drinking the tea.

☰

It made no sense economically or socially to wander the world in 1983. It was counterintuitive, risky even; we could lose it all. But it sounded wonderful. What an enviable position—to be free from entanglements and allegiances.

Banks agreed to come with me if I got a job teaching English somewhere around the world. After all, what were the odds? And if I saw the world, I might learn how to appreciate my hometown cocoon.

Two months later I applied for a job teaching English in Wuhan, China, on the Yangtze River for two years. A teachers university accepted my application quickly. Was that a sign?

Banks gave notice at his firm, where he'd just become the youngest partner. They brought him into a surprise meeting soon after and told him he could leave, effective immediately. Only fools wandered the world when the time was ripe for earning a living and raising a family. Now he had to be committed to the journey.

In a rare quiet moment, I started to rethink what I was proposing. Was traveling going to broaden or narrow my perspective on life? Should we really be doing this? I knew my impulse. When I had beautiful things within grasp, I often threw them away.

Several months later, an envelope with Chinese writing caught my eye in the mail. I set grocery bags on the kitchen counter and opened the letter. An administrator at the university I had applied to in Wuhan, which had a new block-letter name, wrote, "Sorry to inform you, but we changed the name of the university, and your position won't be available for at least another year."

My 1983 passport photo

My 1983 passport stamp

Great! I thought. This gave us more freedom. Why was I so confident this was going to work? I was comfortable with having no idea what we were doing or where we were heading, and the thought of being vagabonds was enticing. But what if we returned as a bag of bones? I was a dreamer who knew no consequences.

I asked Banks how Kathmandu sounded. What would we pack for a trip to Nepal? He brought home the *Lonely Planet* guidebooks and maps, all of which would probably be outdated by the time we arrived halfway around the world.

I didn't need a hair dryer but stuffed my backpack full of toilet paper. I dreaded the idea of ever using my right hand to wipe and left to eat. Or was it vice versa? No way was I abandoning my knife, fork, spoon, toilet tissue, or soap for any reason. Except that I did.

What would bring us home sooner—lack of money or a wane in interest? We planned to take $5,000 in traveler's checks, which was all our savings, and see what called us. Going against the grain and springing for an unending adventure might reap its own rewards.

We ended up traveling eighteen months in Asia by foot, donkey cart, bus top, fourth-class train, riverboat, and camelback. Ironically, when we returned in 1984 we had dodged the Texas real estate bust and had saved more money than if we had stayed in San Antonio. Sadly, some of our friends weren't so fortunate.

All these years later I can calmly reflect on how we turned the public perception of our being senseless to being the smartest couple around for traveling extensively while we were young. On our return I often dressed in my Burmese sarong, and we were in high demand for more than two years to celebrate our story at many public and private organizations.

This trip still feeds me daily, like living water, as I touch again those who touched me. I understand a love for the least out of knowledge, spiritual passion, and adaptive perception. In my twenties, I wanted it all and had imagination but no vision or maturity. I wasn't rebelling against my own culture, just passionate about enlarging it, embracing the world as one body.

Now I look at the wonder of life not only with physical sight but with the "eyes of the heart." *Wishbone: An American Odyssey in Asia* engages other ways of living to unbind prejudices, both others and mine.

Most of the recollections here are taken from the journals and drawings I kept during our travels. It still feels like present tense, though the stories have been changed to past tense for ease of reading. Be my guest in adventure. Look for layers of meaning as we travel these pages together. These words and imagery are not only a record of daily life in the 1980s; they evoke visions of the eternal and the now.

NEPAL

CHINA
NEPAL
Annapurna
Pokhara
Mount Everest
Kathmandu
Sagarmatha National Park
Dharan Bazaar
INDIA

THE GURKHA KNIFE

I asked the Gurkha soldier, now a grandfather, "What is your pleasure in life?"

≡

At 5:30 this morning I was still getting used to rolling the word "Kathmandu" over on my tongue when Banks, my groom of four years, gently spread some burnt orange Tiger Balm on my lips. My nostrils flared; it was like liniment I would put on horse wounds. His mustache was wet from taking a shower, so I wouldn't kiss him with his beads of Kathmandu water. He laughed and said, "Tiger Balm kills amoebas." He was proud of his find from a Tibetan shop in our Kathmandu guesthouse.

≡

We walked down the main dirt road, unable to feel the mountain air yet. Was this street clatter going to accompany us all the way up the mountains? With all of our belongings on our backs, we trudged to catch a bus to Dumre, a one-house town on the trail toward the Annapurnas in the Himalayas, the greatest mountain range on earth. My pack weighed twenty-five pounds, including water; Banks's was about thirty-five. They didn't seem too heavy at first. How naive. Tempa, the Tibetan guide we'd met briefly and hired in a teahouse the day before to take us around the Annapurnas, was not at the bus station. We waited for an hour, until 6:30 a.m., went to Tempa's house, and back to the guesthouse to find he'd been there around 6:15 but had left. We returned to the bus stop and found him sitting patiently on a bench. No way to call. No one had phones.

What a way to begin a three-week relationship of dependency on someone. A rocky start was appropriate to jostle my mind from running on a school-bell schedule. We planned to trek from two thousand feet in Kathmandu to more than seventeen thousand at the highest pass in the Annapurnas, and then back down. This was the beginning of what Banks (who sported a fresh red mustache and beard I'd never seen in the States) and I thought would only be a three-week trek in the Himalayas.

We purchased tickets for the 9:45 bus and went to breakfast. Returned to the station to find that the tickets were actually for an 8:45 bus that had come and gone. Purchased tickets on a local bus, which stopped every ten minutes to pick up chickens, goats, and farmers, and arrived in Dumre five and a half hours later. Felt tedious and mediocre until I shed my Western rhythm for the Eastern tempo. I had to be the one to sync with the environment or remain miserable.

That afternoon we took an open-bed diesel truck filled with rice sacks for four and a half hours through the flatlands. This advanced us two days. A dirt road wound next to the Marsyangdi River and exposed every pothole for the truck to hit. I straddled the rice bags and held on to a loose crossbar. I felt like I was being dipped and scrubbed with dust and a wash bucket. Saw a fox.

After sunset we stopped at a hut halfway through the trip for milk tea. A pet monkey was tied to my wooden bench and wanted my British biscuits. The road cut right across the corner of the hut. The original road had been destroyed for a future bridge. Boards and rocks were placed over a large ditch and then our truck was driven over. The front left tire went through the boards, and the right side of the truck scraped the hut corner. Thank goodness we were still sipping tea with a monkey. The truck was pushed back, boards were straightened, and the vehicle made it across the second time. After bouncing through terraced rice paddies, we reached the road again.

The moon provided brilliant light. Children from villages greeted us and ran along behind, trying to hitch a ride. A long bamboo stick was placed in the back of the truck for any children who grabbed on so they could be batted off.

Many locals walked the road guiding bony buffalo, carrying bundles of sticks, and transporting chickens.

We ate dal bhat (rice and lentils), the staple of the area. I received my first introduction to the Thok Koli people by candlelight. They spoke a Nepalese dialect and seemed very businesslike in manner. They had probably already been exposed to too many Westerners.

Three days later we walked all morning until lunchtime. Spent an hour and a half eating dal bhat and resting in the shade of a woven matted roof. There was no instant food, no McDonalds or feeling of being late. Then we walked another two and a half hours to a spot fifteen minutes outside the next town and decided to camp rather than stay in a teahouse. The stars were bright, and the moon was waxing. We built a fire next to a fast-flowing river and ate crackers and instant soup from New York's Zabar's. We bailed water from the river to put out the fire and watched the moon rise over a small mountain peak. I drifted off the right side of the sliver and fell asleep.

I woke up with my face warm and sprinkled with heavy dew, but my bivouac sack proved itself and kept my body dry. We packed up and walked the one trail to breakfast in town. Who knew how far it really was, but rise after rise Banks was finally enchanted by seeing its sign, Bhu Buhle, and the one teahouse.

"That's the name of our next pet," I said, when we arrived. I immediately took off my rain jacket inside the straw hut.

Banks wasn't thinking of our next pet. He said the steam rising off my back was "quite becoming on me."

Tea and pancakes tasting like warm cookie dough filled our empty stomachs. Tibetan tea consists of yak butter and salt. Definitely not the lowlands milk tea. The Tibetan cooks also boiled water for our two water bottles. I trusted that they boiled it long enough. I was putting my health in the hands of these people.

We climbed steadily again, leaving the fast-flowing river below us but not out of sight. Another town beginning with B was our next night's stay. Stone-shingled clay huts with many windows stretched for miles into the valley. Clouds drifted among the mountains and lifted at times for streams of sunrays.

Banks showed several local girls a tape recorder. Two of them had been singing along the path behind us as we headed to our teahouse. He asked them to sing and played it back on a tape. They were hysterical with laughter. Older locals began to gather around to watch. The next time the girls were asked to sing they became very shy and quiet, turning their backs to the recorder. Banks played their voices back twice as fast, which made them laugh again.

≡

We crossed several memorable suspension bridges. Their architects must have been migrating birds, as sticks were stuffed randomly to make the path. They sprang up, down, and sideways simultaneously. With several people crossing, the bridges felt like trampolines. I was suspended, disoriented, and I couldn't tell where or when they would move beneath me. Everything was in motion—me, the bridge, and the water below. Total suspension.

Several tall trees ahead of us chattered with parrots. They never let us come close to them, moving ahead of us by about thirty feet.

Dal bhat again. There was no menu, no choice. We met a Gurkha who had fought for the British in World War II in Burma. By candlelight, his dark Hindu nature shone as I asked him many questions. I was brash enough to softly ask if he'd killed women and children.

"Yes, I had to," he said. Then he spoke of his personal losses; all three of his brothers and his father had been killed by Germans.

"Was the loss of life on both sides worth it?" I asked.

"No."

British Hindu soldier's Gurkha knife

"What is your pleasure in life?"

He paused and said, "Carrying a burden and living in darkness."

I caught the flash of brass from the Gurkha knife secured to his belt. It was in a leather sheath, but the point protruded slightly at the base of the curve. The knife was the length of his thigh.

"Is your knife for sale?" I said.

"Everything has a price. If you buy it, you will be carrying the blood of many who have felt its edge. You shouldn't ever take it out of the sheath unless you use it." He slowly pulled it partway out of the sheath. I could see the permanent blood stains, layer upon layer, even in the moonlight. "Four dollars."

"Two," I said.

He passed on the knife, which I would carry high and low now through mountain passes. Perhaps he was letting go of one of his burdens, lightening his load as I added to mine. I never even considered how I'd get it back to Texas.

SOME THOUGHTS NOW

All these years later, I still think twice before pulling the knife from its worn leather sheath. Like pulling a wishbone, someone will end up with the short bone. Does blood really need to be shed? For God? For country? Because someone is under duress?

I have wisdom now in the art of the possible. Leadership comes in a desire to increase both freedom and ownership among the group—not subservience, which will ultimately sabotage the work.

Vision has always been my theme, but its definition has broadened for me as I reflect on these travels. I'm a seer of alternatives. Influencing events and inspiring people comes through nurturing, not ordering or demanding. Over time I've gained the capacity for thinking beyond polarities and tapping into full, embodied knowing (which, for me, is prayer). I now tolerate ambiguity, am comfortable with creative tensions, and can finally care for others beyond my own personal advantage.

A ONE-NIGHT CURSE AND CURE

The Tibetan grandmother, owner of the teahouse, was gently stoking the fire and took it upon herself to cure me.

≡

This morning we had tsampa porridge (ground barley, wheat, and corn) and fried eggs on chapatis. We were pleased by a crystal-clear view of Annapurna II and Annapurna III as we followed the Sagarmatha (Everest) National Park map. We traced the Tibetan border for some time, and there were police checkpoints in each town. Tempa, our trusted guide, knew several dialects and told us the exact origin of each group of Tibetans.

≡

As we rose higher in the mountains the terrain became bleaker. There was less variety of food because it had to be brought in by pack mule, and everything was more expensive. One night was three rupees rather than two, assuming we also ate dinner there. Our beds were elevated wooden boards, and if we were especially fortunate these boards would be covered with straw. It was a luxury to have a blanket on top of that.

We spent five and a half hours climbing from 9,000 to 10,500 feet. By the end of the day I felt weaker and had a slight headache, and the last forty-five minutes I was essentially delirious. I just watched the green tennis shoes ahead of me trudging

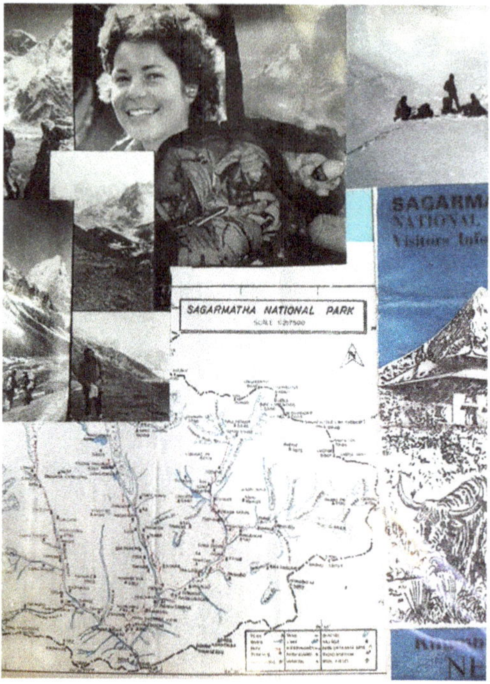

Sagarmatha National Park

through the snow and placed my feet where they had been. This eliminated thinking about where to step. If Banks got too far ahead, I knew I would fall.

We arrived in Pisang and found the second hotel where Alvin, a pig farmer from Prince Edward Island, was staying. We had met him in Kathmandu and then parted ways. An old Tibetan woman owned the house, and two young Tibetan boys worked for her. They were unkempt and washed the dishes in the same fashion, wiping the spoons clean by rubbing them on their pants. They cooked the yak meat to charcoal bits. Because we had never had yak, we didn't know what to expect. Tempa tried it and scolded the boys for burning it. He then cooked some for us. We were offered some yak cheese, which was the consistency of rock candy and tasted like lard. We had potatoes and rice (lowland food) for dinner, which by this time I found unpalatable. Because I was still feeling weak from the day's walk, I decided to go to bed early—but not before we went next door for tea. Five of us climbed up carved tree stumps from the stable to a smoke-filled room and sat around a fire. After we had three cups of tea each, we went back to our hotel.

I went to bed after dinner and experienced all the symptoms of altitude sickness: headache, chills, and nausea. Banks covered me with his sleeping bag and lay on top of me to keep in the warmth. The symptoms passed momentarily.

Tibetan woman who cured me

The next illness I had included severe stomach cramps and a twenty-four-hour process of getting rid of the tsampa porridge I'd eaten for breakfast. I had to walk downstairs on the carved-out totem pole steps to sit by the fire so I would have easy access to the outdoor toilet (anywhere in the snow away from footprints). A Tibetan grandmother, owner of the teahouse, was gently stoking the fire and took it upon herself to cure me. She began telling me about her family in rudimentary English. One son was in jail in Kathmandu, another son ran a shop there, and a third was in the British army. Her husband spent most of his time doing business in Kathmandu. She had emphysema and a goiter in her neck. I was stunned that with all of her hardships she cared for me compassionately and seemed to forget them.

The woman began praying with incantations and her prayer wheel. The wheel spun on a carved brass handle and wheezed slightly as it gained momentum. She sprinkled some cooked rice in the fire and put the rest in a cardboard box. Then she waved this above my head with more pronounced incantations, walked outside, and threw it out. She was exorcizing my illness. I immediately felt worse and ran outside to rid myself of food. I returned weaker than before. She lifted hot coals from the fire on a flat chapati frying pan and had me stare into their blazing core. I felt mesmerized by the glow and the heat as she brought the pan closer to my eyes. I breathed the heat, and then she waved the pan above my head and chanted. She walked outside and threw the coals into the snow. I began to relax.

On an empty stomach I felt good. The woman came in with some chilled wine, a delicacy in those parts, but we couldn't open the bottle without a corkscrew. She told me to heat my hands and press them against my stomach and prepared some strong tea. She massaged my stomach, and soon I fell asleep by the fire.

In the morning I was well. The woman looked pleased and told Tempa that a Tibetan woman we had had tea with yesterday put an evil spell on me because she likes to do this. She was jealous that we were not staying in her teahouse. My healer was very pleased and took credit for exorcizing the evil spirit from me. I had been cursed and cured all in one night. By the time we left Pisang that morning I felt indebted to this kind grandmother who opened her heart and shared her thoughts with us.

As we walked through the snow, Banks told me that another traveler had brought in some hashish the previous evening to smoke through a thin long pipe. The youngest boy wanted to try it, his first experience. He eagerly sucked on the pipe, inhaling so forcefully that it brought the whole wad of hashish through the pipe into his mouth. He became dizzy and burned his lip as he swallowed it. He left the room but apparently survived

Shell-embroidered blouse from same Tibetan woman

the night. On hearing this, I felt his pain more acutely, having just recovered from mine. Most of my pain was anger toward a Westerner's corruption of a youth.

The shell-embroidered blouse my healer wore was one of several she made. I added it to my heavy pack. The difference was that I wanted to carry this burden.

SOME THOUGHTS NOW

In 1983 I was more interested in cultural sharing than biblical text. We carried a Bible then for the historical aspects, and I realized many patterns of living brought the scriptures to life. I approached many wells in the desert with my own camels and saw women congregate around this life spring, this living water. Men rode small donkeys and threatened them with big sticks.

Hindus bow down to many gods and have temples filled with idols, such as the rat temple in India where rats are worshiped and run rampant from huge rice and water bowls. If you see a white rat, it's a good omen.

As I have delved deeper into scripture, my travels live in a new richness. Today I read a passage in Isaiah about exorcising sin through hot coals. I never knew this was a common practice, although it happened to me with a Tibetan grandma in the Himalayas.

This Asian odyssey of more than forty years ago feeds me daily and won't let me go until I share its meaning with others. Perhaps I can create living water, an eternal flow, for all who wish to drink.

When people live in family routines different from their own, they begin to broaden their appreciation for the fact that, no matter how we do it, we are all trying to raise our children and live without strife or harm to ourselves or others. In a sense, as we engage with others we unbind ourselves.

THE YETI SKULL, BURNING CORPSE, AND BALD EVEREST

Descending through four feet of snow along the Thorong La Pass, we would have become frozen statues if we paused for the view at the seventeen-thousand-foot summit. We trudged slowly, then realized we'd lost the trail.

Just a quarter mile ahead, we could see the porter trudging slowly through the snow. We had hired him to break trail and set up camp for $2 a day. We soon passed him and, at about fourteen thousand feet, arrived at a stone shelter as the sun was setting. We immediately jumped into our sleeping bags. I was trying to think positively, reminding myself that we only needed to climb three thousand feet the next day to go over the Annapurna Thorong La Pass.

Then I became hysterical about my toes since I couldn't tell how numb they were. Banks tried to comfort me, saying, "The most famous mountain climbers had fewer than ten toes. You just use corkscrews instead to keep your balance." I laughed, then panicked as I separated my frozen shoe from my frozen neoprene sock, put on dry wool socks, and stuffed myself further into the down bag. We lit candles and lay there thawing out, seven of us snug against each other for shared body heat.

Inside the stone structure were two rooms, one with a fire for cooking and drying socks and shoes, the other for sleeping.

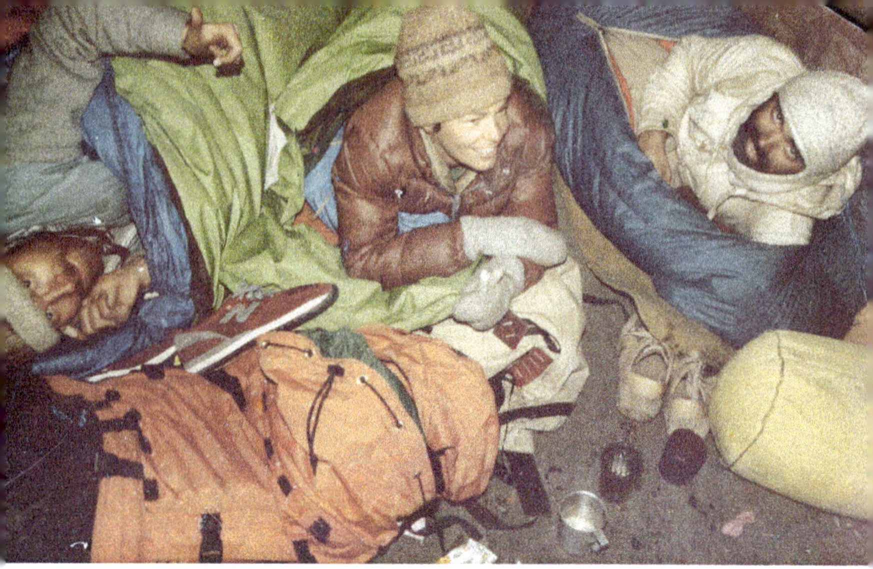

Banks, me, and Wayne in an Annapurna shelter

We swapped international jokes and laughed at our ambition to cross the pass in January.

Tempa and the porter cooked dal bhat and rearranged our tennis shoes and socks for drying close to the fire. We were served dinner in our bags, hot and delicious.

I had on everything I owned—down vest, down jacket, two wool shirts, wool cap, two pairs of wool socks, long johns, wool pants. At times when the wind cut into the shelter through the open door I would sink further into my bag and think of how I might be able to generate more heat.

We woke at 5 a.m. as the world was beginning to turn a glacial blue on the mountain slopes. We had tsampa porridge and chapatis for breakfast. After four cups of tea we broke camp and began a steep climb. After the first seven hundred feet I began crying; I was so cold. Again I thought my toes had frozen, but I knew better than to stop. I had extreme difficulty breathing and felt the fatigue of the climb, fourteen thousand to seventeen thousand feet. We hadn't acclimated except for one day in Manang at eleven thousand feet.

The whole day was a painful push. I was tired, hungry, and dehydrated as I constantly tried to remain awake and alert on the slippery slopes. Ice could be seen below three feet of snowy powder. If I slipped I would skate down about three hundred feet to a frozen river of ice below. There was no ice axe to break my fall. My New Balance tennis shoes provided little traction.

Banks's silhouette against the Himalayas

The night before by the fire, the soles of Banks's tennis shoes had separated from the tops, so he was trying out a new pair. I battled mental fatigue, doubt, and fear, but I couldn't stop. After pushing and fighting for about eight hours we reached the summit (17,800 feet). Tempa had broken a three-foot-deep trail and knew the route by heart; otherwise we would have perished. The wind beat fiercely across the open space and kept us from stopping even to take a picture.

Descending through four feet of snow along the Thorong La Pass, we would have become frozen statues if we paused for the view at the seventeen-thousand-foot summit. We trudged slowly, then realized we'd lost the trail.

≡

Eventually we saw patches of dirt through the snow that revealed the trail. Connecting the patches, we could imagine where the trail curved down the valley. We knew it would become engulfed by cliffs as it deepened. We guessed that it continued on top of the next ridge, so we climbed the snowbank. I sank thigh deep in snow but had learned how to balance and kick steps into it. Our guess was correct, and we followed the trail down to eleven thousand feet to the sparse village of Muktinath, a small police outpost. The sun began to set, but as long as we could see the trail we were not concerned. We were still sliding downhill in ankle-deep snow, and Banks kept slipping and landing bottoms up, since his new tennis shoes had no traction. A tremendous frontal cloud began racing up the mountain. We could see it minutes before it engulfed us and our view of the mountainside. It was humid and warm. We walked through it for ten minutes, and then it was suddenly behind us, leaving as rapidly as it came. We had a clear view of the mountains again. We were sliding, skating, skiing down thousands of feet. Our energy was high because we were at last on our way to a place where we could relax.

Darkness beat us to Muktinath. We traveled by night for at least an hour, though Tempa said we had only fifteen more minutes. At last we were in the lowlands. Four of us traveled by flashlight; the other five had descended more quickly and were probably in a warm teahouse. Alvin, second in line behind Tempa, was telling us there was a rock on the right and ice straight ahead. It was clearly the blind leading the blind. We arrived at Muktinath about 7:15 p.m. after a twelve-hour walk. The hotel had previously been owned by policemen, and seven of them gathered around a stove and a kerosene-generated light waiting for dal bhat. The accommodations were the best in Muktinath, and we felt triumphant telling them our story of the pass.

≡

We ordered every hot drink available and egg-vegetable fried rice. The vegetables were fresh and the variety outstanding after coming off a harsh, bleak mountain. After refreshing ourselves with food and drink, we hit the bed for a solid night's sleep.

The next morning we left Muktinath at 6:45 a.m. for a five-and-a half-hour walk before the wind swept up the valley. The winds started around 11 a.m.

We stopped in Kagbeni, a medieval village with narrow alleyways and wooden ladders leading to hidden places. It was a stone blockade built at the confluence of two rivers. Long ago a king controlled commerce in all directions from this location, but a mud castle was all that remained. What a great name for my next dog: Beni for short.

Blue sheep (so called because they blended into the icy blue terrain), a rare sighting, appeared on a ledge on our way down the range to Jomsom. This commercial town had no atmosphere, only an airport. Travelers could easily walk here from Kathmandu without much effort. We were heading toward fruit country; in Jomsom the teahouses offered fresh apple pie.

The wind was fierce around 1 p.m., so we were delighted to sit and watch "Borax mule" teams clang by. Donkeys and cows were loaded down with rice sacks. Bells and banners bedecked them to make them more active (noise and peripheral flap energize them). Every place we stopped had a picture of the king and queen of Nepal. The pictures were draped in a thin white scarf to show endearment and respect.

We visited a Buddhist temple exhibiting colorful gold-faced Buddhas protected by orange saffron-robed monks. The paintings on the steep walls were brilliant symbols of long-lasting life: flowers, vessels, fish, and so on. Although the monastery allowed us to visit the inner courtyard, we couldn't go into the inner sanctum (especially true for a woman). We were told we could view a yeti skull for five rupees. It sounded intriguing and suspicious to me, but we paid the fee. A monk took us upstairs to a chest, unlocked it, and opened it slowly. Inside was a black piece of leather the size of half a football. Bright orange coarse hair two inches long, sticking straight out, was attached to the outside. We had read about such things from various sources, including the San Antonio Zoological Society; most thought it might be part of an old goat.

I hadn't been able to bathe for a week. I kept my clothes snug to my body in the hopes that I was the only one to smell myself. It was extremely hard to keep clean around wood fires and dirt floors.

We stayed in a teahouse frequented by Westerners in Marpha, a town as stark as the town of Marfa in West Texas. Five guys sitting around the fire were having a lively conversation, unaware of their environment and the clanging mule teams passing by the window. A young Nepalese cook said that in fifteen days the western side of the Annapurnas (the Muktinath side) would be overrun with Westerners; it was prime tourist season. The teahouse held twenty-five people but could house up to forty with many sleeping downstairs on the floor by the fire.

The fruits and vegetables and starches came from Pokhara by mule team.

We visited another Buddhist monastery that morning. The head Buddha's face had a fiery-red demonic expression. There were the usual large Tibetan drums along with clarinet-type horns and conch shells, played simultaneously and followed by chanting.

The next morning while I was sipping a Coke in a hilltop teahouse, a corpse almost brushed me off the trail. Four men rushed by with a body on a stretcher of linen on bamboo poles. We fell in behind the procession down the hill to the waterfall. I tried to blend in like a boulder while we observed the cremation. Men piled rocks to form a pit near the water about four feet deep. Other men chopped trees down from the hillside close by for wood to pile on top of the pit. Women were crouched in the boulders with their mouths covered, preparing to mourn.

The corpse waited patiently to be freed from its impurities; water would carry the ashes away. The body, a woman's, was dressed in linen with roses. A Nepali at her head and another at her feet moved her around the pit twice in an irregular circle. Then she was placed on top of the pyre and wood was thrown on top of her except for her face. A blaze began beneath her, and the linen was consumed immediately, exposing the skin and hair. The skin began to burn, exposing a white skull. The skull became charred. The fire stokers began celebrating by offering us the first drink of their homemade rakshi (local rice wine). I pretended to drink, Banks really did, the bottle was passed, and cigarettes were smoked. I felt certain that Banks would pay for that with a strange illness in our next country.

A few people wailed, but most were smiling. The bottle was filled from a gallon container and brought to us when a quarter was left. We were told to finish it. Three bottles came to us that way. By this time we were all smiling and celebrating. I asked if I could take pictures, and they said that would be fine. Sixteen shots later I ran out of film. A Gurkha started poking the body, crunching it down into the hot blaze. An hour and a half later we said we had to go and bid them namaste. We saw the smoke rise from the valley to the mountaintop.

We visited a Tibetan refugee camp on our way out of Marpha. The Tibetans seemed desperate for rupees for the coming Tibetan new year on February 12. They would celebrate for one week solid and close all their shops. Wood was piled three to four feet high on the tops of flat houses, aged because it had been cut by fathers, grandfathers, even great-grandfathers. The current families wouldn't use this old wood due to the expectation that each Marphan family should chop their own.

Tempa told us that many things were destroyed in Tibet during the Chinese Cultural Revolution. We went to his friend's house for Tibetan tea. He described excellent-quality coral as having deep red eyes. Women and men wore coral and turquoise necklaces and earrings and passed them down through the family. I offered my down vest in trade for some coral earrings. The Tibetan was interested in it for its practical value. He tried it on and zipped it up. We couldn't agree on a price, so we nodded namaste to each other and parted ways.

Finding toilets at night was a risky business. Every evening I was in a new place that was several stories high. I felt my way down totem-pole ladders to the stable and along the wall to the latch on the stable door. If I didn't feel a horse's muzzle or step on a baby goat I knew I'd make it out the door. That night I walked downstairs to where the mules were munching in the dark. I started to pull up my skirt and squat when I heard a trickling behind me. Someone else had the same idea, but neither of us could see the other. I waited. A man appeared in the moonlight and climbed back up the ladder.

The women stoked the fires here since they prepared meals. Afterward they took splinters from the wood and used it as dental floss or stimulants to clean their teeth.

The previous night I had dreamed I was sleeping on a camel's back. I woke to realize my bed was made of straw that arched in the center.

I heard bells clanging and opened my windows to look down on a mule team of dzos (a hybrid of domestic cattle and yaks).

We traveled for five hours, and I thought about Marpha. The village was getting electricity in a week. Locals constantly flipped wall switches with pride, even though nothing was connected yet. Every space had been wired, and people walked around talking about it. They were waiting for hydroelectricity from Jomsom. Hot showers would be a bonus.

☰

That afternoon we arrived at Mustang Lodge. I walked through the front door to find at least ten Western faces, all silent, their eyes staring at me. It was a culture shock to see so many Westerners at once—the most we'd seen in one place on our travels.

We put down our packs and wandered through the town. We started following some young boys through green wheat fields and over stone walls. They carried baskets filled with dung on their backs and were laughing and singing. At the top field they emptied the dung into a pile, turned, and met us. "Hello, mitai. Give me your pen," they said. We both laughed at their familiar greetings to Westerners. I then put an empty basket on my back and used the head strap to balance. The basket jostled since there was no weight in it. The boys laughed at my awkwardness. We started humming together as I led the way down the hill to the village. I cleared the top of a stone wall nicely and started down the totem-pole ladder. A jump to the bottom knocked my wool cap into my eyes. I kept walking, which also made the boys laugh. We entered the stable where women scooped dung into the baskets for them to carry to the fields.

We began walking again around 9:30 a.m. when the mule teams finished passing through town. I was right behind the driver and the last three mules. He beat the last one, forcing the two in front to bunch. They jockeyed for footing and the outside one lost. He dropped back and grasped the slate curb with his front hooves but tumbled head over heels three hundred feet to the river bottom. He kicked to get up but could only raise his head. The head driver was furious at the back driver's carelessness and the loss of a six-thousand-rupee mule. "Now what can you do with a dead mule?" he yelled, and loosened the rice bags and saddle and made the other driver carry it.

Ξ

Locals carrying sixty to seventy kilos were a common sight as well as smell. The stench surrounding them resulted from the healthy, smoky fires they sat beside night after night, which absorbed into their skin.

Children up to age six wore skirts, no pants. Why?

Ξ

Fires were the center of life here. They provided heat in cold stone houses and light where darkness otherwise prevailed.

After rising for one and a half hours, from 7,700 feet, we rounded a ridge at 9,200 feet. There before us stood Mount Everest, or as the Nepalese called it, Sagarmatha, in its clear, momentary splendor. As we watched, a long frontal system swept over it, concealing it from view.

We stopped at an apple house and had some cider and then continued to climb on a trail with stones laid out to lead us. A cheese factory at the pass made a delicious Swiss-type cheese that only tourists could afford.

Last night the Sherpa stew was excellent: beans, noodles, carrots, cabbage, potatoes, and spinach. The apple pancakes were lightly cooked like crepes.

We spent eight and a half hours walking along precipices overlooking a gorge. The view was spectacular, which helped us toward the end when we grew very tired. Wild orchids blossomed along waterfalls. The trail was a rollercoaster for at least nine ridges. It started raining in the last hour, and we kept hoping to see the village ahead. Finally we topped one more rise to find the town below. We stopped at another Sherpa house, put on dry clothes, and were brought black tea (no sugar) to warm us. It was only 3 p.m., and we had been traveling since 6:45 that morning. We spread out our bags and had plenty of light for reading. About an hour later Wayne, our Australian lifeguard friend, came busting through the door. It was fun to reminisce about our coldest night bundled together on the Thorong La Pass.

Namche Bazaar, a town named after its market, was easy to find the next day. The trail was broad and rose gradually, except for a steep climb the last hour. We made it in five hours and had time to rent boots and down jackets (six rupees a day). I asked a woman if she had sanitary napkins, and she didn't understand at first. Then she pulled out a bag with a diaper inside. I pointed to myself, and she cut it lengthwise into strips. I bought it for two rupees along with some ginger snaps.

I was famished. First I had muesli, then fried rice with vegetables, fresh bread, and a piece of chocolate cake. I still wanted food, so I had Sherpa stew and noodles with vegetables.

The night before, we met a Japanese man and his Nepalese interpreter. He was researching high blood pressure in Nepal to compare it with the populations in Japan. He recorded how much Tibetan tea (yak butter and salt again) the locals drank and took their blood pressure. Blood pressure was typically very low in Nepal, even though the people drink large quantities of tea with salt and sugar. He also took my blood pressure (which was 114) and my pulse (78).

We had seen a yak the night before that was saddled and waiting patiently in a pasture. I had a great urge to ride him, and he seemed like prime game. I walked up to him and tried to grab the string around his neck. He turned toward me with his curly horns and tried to rend me. Might made right here, so I eased away.

≡

Today we had a pleasant climb from Namche to Pangboche (11,400 to 12,800 feet). I loved the names of these towns because they were rhythmic and had no meaning in my language. There were many yaks here but no curd to be found. We climbed through grassy highlands looking down on glacier-carved riverbeds and passed through more pastures and herds of yaks. Banks passed one yak and pulled its tail gingerly. It kicked its leg out swiftly; thank goodness, his aim was poor. We pushed on to 14,000 feet, as it was still early afternoon, and sat in the sun enjoying the view of Nuptse and wondering what Everest looked like directly behind it.

As more people ventured up to the only lodge open, it became extremely crowded. Just below the lodge a Tibetan woman with two yaks arrived and opened a second lodge. We took advantage of the opportunity to be in a more spacious place and joined her. She had just returned from Namche, where her husband had recently been killed in a fight with three men. Her six-year-old son was staying with her father. She explained to us that her luck was no good. Her brother, however, had successfully climbed Everest three times. She unloaded large boxes of supplies she had brought from the Everest base camp. They were from the 1982 Canadian expedition, and she had transported them here by yak. Her shelves were stocked full of cheeses, peanuts, mixed fruits, French creams, canned fruits, and sardines. We could also pick out foods from other expeditions and determine how old the cans were. For example, there were many Spanish products dated 1981 from an Everest expedition.

We ate Sherpa stew with rice, onion, and green collards and had rice pudding for dessert. Then the woman made yak brain stew with two-month-old meat for herself. The longer the meat was left in the snow, the better. She added chili powder and offered us a small portion. I lifted the spoon to my mouth, and the smell overpowered me. It reminded me of liver that had been left out on the counter for several days. It tasted strong and seemed to have the ability to cure an illness with its potency. Banks and I crunched on part of the brains, which I described in my journal as "spongy but granular; sticky, yet mushy like bread pudding."

≡

I had rented some overshoes in Namche that were made in 1951. My running shoes fit loosely inside, and I strapped them through rings on the outside so the overboot fit snugly to the shoes. They must have been size eleven, because there was ample room in the toes.

The previous day had been socked in. It snowed the night before and was cloudy, especially in the direction of Everest. We rested all day, reading, writing, and drinking black tea. We were slightly disappointed at the weather after traveling so far in such a short time, but the next morning was crystal clear. We were elated by the clarity of the surrounding mountains.

We walked over occasional boulder-covered glaciers that popped above the surface ten or twelve feet. The land was gnarled and scarred from glacial movement. It looked as if fifteen bulldozers had dug in haphazard directions. One glacial formation looked like a miniature Himalayan range. Other sections looked like the pipes of cathedral organs. Glaciers surrounded the mountains, carving or chiseling them down. For two hours we walked across these boulder-covered glaciers, seeing deep crevasses filled with frozen water and rock.

A rare clear view of Sagarmatha

The last hour was a steep climb from around 17,000 to 18,192 feet. I had to take short steps and found myself breathing heavily the entire way. The ground was easy to maneuver, for large boulders supplied easy footing. Banks made it in two and a half hours and was waiting at the top with the camera tucked away in his coat to keep it from freezing.

The 360-degree view from the top of Kala Patthar was spectacular. The were at least fifteen mountains, all higher than Mount McKinley in North America (20,320 feet). In every direction a jagged, majestic mountain expressed its own beauty and might. Everest was a black rock against a foreground of the Khumbu icefall with Lhotse to its left and an unnamed shoulder to its right. It was like a huge mammoth rising from a snow pit for a breath of fresh air. I could pick out the traditional South Col route that the Canadian expedition took. I thought of our friend who would be climbing it from the Tibetan side. I later read that most of the expeditions before 1950 were British and attempted Everest from the Chinese side until Nepal opened its borders. I finally photographed a panoramic series by taking a few shots, then tucking the camera into my down jacket to thaw. The wind blew fiercely on top, and at times I huddled among boulders to break its chill.

During my coldest moments I thought about Khumbu, which would be my next black cat's name. Kagbeni and Khumbu. I was acquiring quite a household.

I raced down the mountain to a flat sandy desert valley. We proceeded back to Lobuche for chapatis and apricot jam and then walked one and a half hours to Pheriche. The weather turned cloudy and windy. It began to snow slightly. I enjoyed walking through a valley of yaks with brushy heather at my feet and flowing brooks at my side.

The next morning I woke around 6 a.m. to a clear view of the mountains. Banks and I walked back to Dingboche to capture a view of Island Peak. We crested hills and passed yaks being herded to the high pastures. On our way back to Pheriche a scampy dog licked our heels and scared yaks away.

In Pheriche we visited the outpatient clinic to talk to a doctor from New York. He couldn't give us much information about the States, though he had just arrived the day before.

When we got back to Namche we visited a three-hundred-year-old gompa with a seven-foot prayer wheel that sounded a bell. This bell signaled a lama who lived at the top of the hill. From the sound he knew there were visitors and within ten minutes arrived with a key. There were two levels to this gompa, both with intricate paintings and three-foot statues of the Buddhas and female divinities. Three-foot Tibetan drums and scarves hung from the ceilings.

We went upstairs to find large demonic masks on the walls. The lama asked us if we would like to see a yeti scalp and hand. After we said yes, he asked for money. Banks gave him ten rupees, and the lama pointed to me, indicating that I needed to pay too. Then he unlocked a wooden chest and pulled out a second chest and a small box. It contained a black object, which was a half-inch-thick scalp. What a proud moment for the lama, who tapped the scalp a few times to show us its strength. He then uncovered and opened the box. A gnarled, shrunken hand lay limply inside. He picked it up and turned it so we could see that it still had a little meat on it. The middle finger was curled under and solid black.

Sometime later, as I was glancing through a registry, I came upon a cover page detailing research done in 1958 by the San Antonio Zoological Expedition. A letter by Peter Byrne explained that the so called yeti hand was actually a human hand. There was no full explanation for the scalp, however. The two pieces were impressive enough to me no matter what they were.

≡

We began walking down the one trail to Kathmandu. Ridges stretched out before us. As we conquered one we found another just as majestic before us. It began to snow lightly, and the clouds dropped, covering us as well as the ridges. Snow had melted into mud on some parts of the trail. As we rounded a bend of snow-covered ridges, I saw an iridescent Himalayan monal (danphe, the national bird) roaming the scrub. He was gorgeous against the snow light. Banks and I saw two more soon after that, especially the silhouetted topknot of one.

We passed many yaks heavily laden with items for sale in Namche Bazaar the following Saturday. Two of the women we stayed with in Lobuche and Pheriche were accompanied by yaks.

We finally got back to Namche. I returned my 1951 classic boots, and we had fresh bread, hot from the oven, to satisfy our tummies.

We had passed all the people we had spent nights with on our way up. Most were gathered in Tengboche to acclimate for several days. They thought we were extraordinary because we had climbed from 2,410 to 18,192 feet in eight days. We had fried yak momos and pasta cakes with them and said goodbye.

It was pleasant to encounter Wayne, our Aussie friend, again in Namche.

≡

The moon was bright and beaming through my second-story window. I arose around 6 a.m. to read *Born in Tibet*. About an hour and a half later smoke began to fill the room as the Sherpa mother started the juniper fire. Banks and I started the morning with black tea and pancakes, porridge, and chocolate cake.

That Saturday we wandered over to the market around 11 a.m. to see crowds of people, Tibetan and Nepalese, bartering and selling their rice, corn, millet, meat, and biscuits. The market was situated along a ridge in Namche, and people crowded through the narrow pathways. Wayne and the American doctor we had met earlier, Richard, stationed themselves above the crowds so they could capture the scene with their telephoto lenses. I milled around among the bargainers and snapped shots of weathered elderly Tibetan men. They wore turquoise and coral earrings and necklaces; some wore Teddy Roosevelt hats, black, round, and stubby.

≡

I stood by the raw meat of a freshly butchered buffalo whose head remained with the meat so people knew what they were buying. I bought fifteen tangerines for ten rupees (eighty cents). It took half an hour to do this. Two Westerners were also there and spoke Nepalese, which aided greatly in the bargaining. Speaking the language of the country I was in would break so many barriers, but I would need to know Mandarin, Cantonese, Urdu, Farsi, Nepalese, and Thai!

≡

A young woman in a Namche shop wanted to buy my jacket before we went into the mountains. Banks rented a cheap Chinese down jacket from her, and she offered to purchase mine for 700 rupees (fifty dollars) when we returned. The morning we returned the jacket, she offered 550 rupees for mine. I explained why my jacket was top quality, demonstrating the durable zipper and Velcro pockets stuffed with down. The material was ripstop nylon, and the roll collar kept me warmer. We parted with her offering us some Mai Tai beer, and I walked out appreciating my jacket even more.

Banks and I wandered over to the bakery and bought two loaves of bread hot out of the oven. I stuck them between my wool shirts, and they warmed my upper torso as we walked in the brisk wind. We meandered around town, snooping among houses away from the main shopping area. An old Sherpa woman came out of a basement area, and Banks noticed her Tibetan shoes. I said "Kati" ("How much?") and pointed to her scuffy boots. She began yelling in Nepalese to a woman upstairs, and soon a granddaughter appeared with some new Tibetan boots with yak-skin bottoms and yak and sheep wool tops. They wanted 200 rupees; we bought them for 180 (twelve dollars).

Several days later we left Namche Bazaar for an eight-hour walk with extreme ups and downs as we descended out of the Himalayas, including devilish forests where the trail had been washed out in places, leaving a fifty-foot cliff to negotiate. In one ominous forest I stepped on a loose root that jutted out like the gnarled yeti hand we had seen in Pangboche. The night before, in Karte, a mangy mutt had yelped for the first hour of dusk. Local Nepalese porters slept in the same room and hacked through the night, likely the result of being close to too many fires for too many years. The roof leaked on our friend Wayne; I could hear the drops spatter on his sleeping bag.

The next town was no longer Sherpa or Tibetan. The people were Hindu Nepalese. The men wore Nepalese caps and baggy pants that cinched at the ankles, and the women wore nose rings, blouses that tied on the left with sashed middles, and wrapped skirts. The animals seemed healthier in the lower lands. The dogs no longer had matted, mangy fur but shiny coats and sparkly eyes. A fat rabbit roamed free in one of the stores.

The days were getting hotter as we went southward and downward. I missed the cool mountain air and dramatic dips and climbs of the previous two weeks. The landscape was flattening out, leaving me depressed. The dress was heavily influenced by Indian styles. A few men wore short and long skirts, and several wore only a loincloth. The women wore colorful scarves. We stopped to eat lunch in a small village. The only teahouse was opposite a school where classes were being held outside.

As the children saw us arrive, they abandoned their teachers and formed a row across the path from us to stare. By the time thirty children had gathered in silence I felt I needed to perform to make it worth stopping class for me. I clapped a tune similar to rat-a-tat-tat to see if they could follow. They tried shyly to clap. Banks began writing on a bench outside the teahouse. This encouraged and intrigued them, and they gathered around to see if they could read the English. I looked into the mass of eyes, and the children laughed and ran for cover if they felt my presence too strongly. Then a whole section followed like sheep. They were endowing me with more power than I wished.

That afternoon we caught a bus for another four-hour ride to Kathmandu. A man we met on the bus invited us to stay in his flat-topped house on the outskirts of Patan. His family was building the home themselves; three out of five rooms were done. He had a loving family of six children. We were shown a comfortable bed, and then our friend began preparing rice and vegetables on three kerosene stoves. He used special, clean lard and explained that vegetable oil was quite dangerous because contaminated lots were knowingly sold by the ton to Nepal from India. It was a major cause of hepatitis.

Our friend's purpose in life seemed to be defined by his family. "Why do you have such a large family?" I said.

"My children are representatives of my wife and me in case we die young," he said.

He seemed impressed that I liked the family's size and that the children were helpful and caring with each other. Where, I wondered, was the bickering and strife I experienced in my own childhood? The youngest, a ten-month-old, was the center of attention for all of the children. A teenage girl, the sister of one of the son's girlfriends, was retained to cook and clean in exchange for room and board. During the day she attended school, pressing her green school uniform each morning. The iron was the only appliance I saw in the home. Outside the house were a healthy vegetable garden and a clean outhouse. Our friend took us up on the rooftop in the morning, and we oriented ourselves to the surroundings with a map.

He was frank with us about politics and the lack of freedom of speech and action in Nepal. The powerful controlled the court system. A Nepalese must always publicly praise the government, proclaiming that fairness and justice existed for all. But life, our friend said, was uncertain for anyone who spoke out against the status quo. Privately, in small groups, Nepalese could canvass their oppression without risking their own or their families' lives.

In the morning we had fresh vegetables with clean white rice. Hot milk was our wholesome dessert. Our friend offered us genuine hospitality. His family had the minimum to exist on but also a great reservoir of love. This man had an *Oxford English Dictionary* at his bedside. He had been taught impeccable English by British instructors and used his education to create a dignified lifestyle in a barren land.

In this manner we were welcomed back to Kathmandu. We reverted to our decadent lifestyle after leaving our friend, spending rupees on books, magazines, and rich foods. I appreciated that Nepalese man's philosophy of life; by comparison I was a corrupted Westerner.

We stayed in Kathmandu for a week, recuperating and indulging in the variety of foods and people. I finished the novel *A Passage to India*, which offered exotic descriptions of the land, strong characters, and the intense interrelationship between the two. The obstacles people surmounted in order to meet others of different cultural backgrounds had called up generous, provocative minds.

Beggars were a big market in Kathmandu. Children were coerced into having a limb cut off for business purposes. They saw only about a tenth of the money they earned begging. The rest went to the person who cut off the limb.

Nepalese seemed to accept life's incongruities and hardships and even celebrated death because of their belief in reincarnation.

We sold our self-inflating Therm-a-Rest pads for seventy dollars. As a Tibetan woman gave us the bills, she explained the difference between real and counterfeit money. At the time an expedition porter happened to be standing in her secondhand store with Bangkok dollars—counterfeits. He openly demonstrated the difference. I trust we weren't given counterfeit bills, although I still couldn't tell the difference. We had bought the Therm-a-Rests new for $100 in New York. This was not a bad trade, and it really lightened my load.

I sold my running shoes for twenty rupees ($1.40). They leaked, the soles were starting to come off, and the bottoms were worn at an extreme angle, but a secondhand equipment store found a reason to buy them. We sold our plastic measuring cups for ten rupees, which would buy us two large pots of milk tea. I sold my Gore-Tex waterproof pants for a hundred rupees ($7). They were about four years old, had a grease smudge on the rear, and were beginning to crinkle around the crotch. Besides, they weren't the right size for me, too broad in the waist and too short. That's what I got for buying through the mail. I sold several books. We could get half the price we paid if we sold them to the original store. *Kama Sutra*, *A Passage to India*, *Trekking in Nepal*, *Kim*, and *King Solomon's Mines* together brought eighty-seven rupees ($6.50).

The previous night Banks and I had visited our Nepalese friend and his family again. We took him four colored pens, some English newspapers, and an American magazine. The pens were a hit with his children. The younger daughter became very possessive of them, saying who could use what color and for how long.

I sketched a rabbit that was in a cage next to me and encouraged her to draw it. I thought she would look at the rabbit, but she looked at my drawing and tried to copy it. Then I drew a picture of her and wanted her to draw me. She shyly declined, but one of her brothers readily accepted. He started over about three times before drawing a face with curly hair.

We had dal bhat for dinner. Our friend—I never could pronounce his name—ate with his fingers while squatting over a low platform. He gingerly mixed the lentils with his rice and scooped them into his mouth. It was a pleasure to see him eat.

Yesterday we went to Trick Street, an area of Kathmandu that thrived on old hippies in the 1960s. It was still the town's drug haven. We were approached every few minutes by Nepalese asking if we wanted smack, cocaine, and hashish or to change money. We went into a cosmopolitan restaurant crowded with Westerners staring into space. Most were either already high or passing around bongs and hashish joints. Nepalese masks on the walls were lit up with Christmas tree lights. The music had a fast disco beat. I went downstairs to the "toilet" and saw three guys sniffing cocaine in the hallway.

Today we sold our mini cassette recorder for six hundred rupees (forty-two dollars). It was new, had not been used much, and had five cassettes and earphones. We hadn't registered it when we came into Nepal, so there was no government record. Had there been one, we would have paid heavy taxes.

Yesterday I spent the morning in bed or at the toilet. By afternoon I was able to go out. Food poisoning, I supposed.

Bhim Birag, a singer and composer of music for Radio Nepal, showed us around the broadcasting studio today. We walked past an armed military guard who questioned our Nepalese friend before letting us pass. Entering a small room on the left, we found musicians practicing for a recording. A woman played a sitar, a man sang and played a harmonium (similar to an accordion), and another person tapped on a drum, the national instrument of Nepal. In the control room we saw the musicians recording a national song. All broadcasting seemed to be patriotic, and Radio Nepal was their only broadcasting system. A Japanese had financed and constructed a new building for Radio Nepal next to the existing one. Birag recorded sad love songs, perhaps a result of losing his wife in an accident. They were walking down the street when a motorcycle hit them, killing her and destroying Birag's legs.

Sitting on the steps of Durbar Square, which led up to a Hindu temple, I watched street vendors and Western consumers bargain. An Indian dressed in white suddenly appeared before me displaying a book of compliments to himself "for his ear cleaning ability and soothing massages." For twenty rupees I succumbed to curiosity. I suppressed my apprehension as he stuck sharp metal instruments into my delicate ears. After digging the wax loose, he used long slender tweezers to pull wads of wax from my ears. It felt as if he was pulling inner skin from them. I didn't question the sanitary methods. He collected the wads of wax on his finger and displayed them proudly for me. I had to admit, the quantity was impressive. He finished by poking his forefingers in both ears and popping them out like corks off a wine bottle. My hearing seemed more acute, as if he had opened holes in my head. I left the balls of wax with him, though I could have easily made a candle out of them. I wondered if he collected wax from all around the world. One problem with having clean ears was that I could hear traffic noise more acutely, and there was plenty of it.

As we were preparing to leave, we received two floral leis from our favorite bookstore, good-luck charms from the locals. Tempa's wife gave us good-luck scarves similar to the ones that framed the king and queen's pictures in shops and homes. We also went to Jamaly's, our most frequented restaurant, for quiche and salad. They gave us free brownies as going-away presents. The Nepalese are generally very hospitable.

≡

We began a course of Fansidar malaria pills, the type most Westerners take for Thailand, Burma, and Malaysia, and would continue taking them weekly.

We sold twelve packages of Lipton's instant tomato soup for fifteen rupees, which allowed Banks to buy a pair of flip-flops that were more practical. We bought the latest issues of *International Herald Tribune* (ten rupees), *Asia Week* (seventeen rupees), and the *Times of India* (one rupee). For a Nepalese this would be quite a luxury. Our Nepalese friend could not afford them. He spent about seventy rupees a day feeding a family of eight. His daily salary was around thirty-five rupees, his wife's as a secretary was fifteen to twenty, and one son's was ten. This barely covered the cost of basic needs. Their ten-month-old baby had the highest expenses since they bought powdered milk at thirty-seven rupees a can; they spent three hundred to four hundred rupees a month on milk alone.

At the Kathmandu airport we bought two bottles of Teacher's instead of Johnnie Walker Black because the duty-free shop was out of it. We got Benson and Hedges (two cartons) instead of 555 cigarettes. From hearsay Johnnie Walker Black and 555 were the best to sell on the black market in Burma.

We walked the streets of Kathmandu once more and saw a middle-aged man who used his leg to walk on, though it was gangrened from toe to thigh. The foot, ankle, and calf were three times the size of his other limb.

The meat shops displayed buffalo and goat meat for sale. The meatier parts had center stage on the floor, with intestines, bones, heads, and legs pushed to the side. All of the meat sat in a pool of blood where it had been chopped. The goats were cured in an orange solution; their orange heads stunned me as they stared back at me glassy-eyed.

We went to the national museum, which was celebrating King Tribhuvan, a monarch of Nepal at the age of six. The palace architecture was more impressive than its contents, which included a great many pictures of the king visiting other countries. His clothes were well preserved, the desk utensils nicely polished. Even his favorite birdcage was intact, with his favorite canary, stuffed, inside. All was preserved except him. He was as wealthy as a middle-class American.

I could tell my ears were clean because they didn't crackle, just popped, at high altitudes on Biman Airways (Burmese) jets. On the Russian-made imitation American plane called a Fokkor F28, "Your life vest is under your seat" was written twice in English and once in Burmese.

At present we were in Dacca, Bangladesh, en route to Rangoon. We were unable to leave the plane since there was only a thirty-minute layover.

Wisdom and compassion for the existing world were two virtues I hoped to acquire through my travels. I wanted to be as wise as the serpent and as gentle as the dove. Part of gaining wisdom was meeting all kinds of people and being able to judge their integrity before taking what they said to heart. Oral tradition was the most important means of communication in Asia; the printed page was always out of date. We found things out by questioning people who had just been where we were going. "He who speaks does not know; he who knows does not speak," to quote a famous Buddhist.

Another aspect of wisdom was the ability to remain untouched or tainted by the knowledge acquired. So why did I want to become enlightened?

≡

SOME THOUGHTS NOW

I've always fed myself from this wishbone. I am in love with the East, but I live in the West. Years after our travels, Banks and I divorced, so part of me was lost. But at some point I found a container stored high in the garage, filled with my Asian sketchbooks.

Who would read their journals from forty years ago? Why think about the people we passed going up or down a mountain? We were all in transition in one way or another. Weren't we?

I loved sharing with strangers in a world of scarce resources. The environment's hardy character brought its own riches of interdependence. I think daily about Nepal's challenging landscape, which forced us to depend on one another. It reminded me of Alaska, where I spent the first five years of my life. People helped without asking what religion or nationality someone was. They helped even when they had opposing views. We seemed to have an unstated agreement that we were all one blood, and life mattered. I interpret that as Christ's message to love one another.

I still think of the Gurkha, the Tibetan women, and the travelers we lived with for weeks at a time. The Gurkha grandfather had a change of heart late in life. The Tibetan mothers and grandmothers were capable business managers, cooks, and cleaners, skilled at sharing with foreigners. The Tibetan men were noticeably absent. Did women really run the culture as a basic matriarchy? I thought of the Chinese matriarchy early in their history before the dynasty wars. What would the world be like if women were the ones to decide whether to kill or love our differences away? Am I still naive?

I remember the French who had to be airlifted from the top of the Annapurna pass where we huddled in a stone hut in mid-January. They lost some of their toes to frostbite. I wore neoprene socks and tennis shoes, and the sole separated from Banks's shoes left near the fire to dry. We were all naive together.

I wonder where Alvin and his Swiss girlfriend, Ruth (now his wife), are? We had spent several days with them, and they talked about starting a farm a mile from Alvin's father's house on Prince Edward Island to raise their own pigs. What about the Aussie Wayne and the German Karl? The American Kathy? We carried each other's loads and then let go. But the caring remained.

≡

My friend Jennifer got back from Nepal a week ago. She was visiting Nepalese friends she had met ten years earlier when she was trekking around the Annapurnas. She, too, bonded in what seemed like happenstance encounters there. Her love of the land and people is with her daily.

We met a year ago and have been linked in comradery through our stories of eating dal bhat and loving the mystery of a hardy people. We both work to embrace diversity and have formed a group of like-minded spirits.

Jennifer tells me that Kathmandu is now extremely overpopulated with many from the mountains who have escaped a recent earthquake. This, mixed with tourists inundating the city, has created so much pollution that breathing masks are highly recommended.

The small village is now a Bangkok or New Delhi. The smog drifts over to Pokhara by the lake twenty miles away, where a new airport is being built. At the moment, I have no desire to return. I'd rather keep the memories rippling through rivers in my mind.

My Episcopal sisters in New Braunfels, Texas, 2018

INDIA

RIDING HUMPBACKS IN THE DUNES

Camels sifted through flat sands in a bedroom slipper shuffle.

Jaisalmer is a sleepy sandcastle undulating above the wavy, blinding Thar Desert in northern Rajasthan, India. The day before we had wandered into a tea shop (everything happens there) and met two young camel jockeys who spoke broken English. We hired them to serve as our guides for ten days—and 223 miles—in the dunes. By the time we finished it was settled: shifting dunes, rickety camels, and our trust in guides we had just met seemed natural.

Today around 9 a.m. we sauntered into the flat western plain. Burlap bags full of grass for the camels, eight blankets, and a vegetable bag for us were roped atop a two-person saddle. I chose the front seat, throwing my leg over my camel Saree's shoulder as he knelt on all fours.

Jaisalmer, Punjab, India

Familiarity came quickly between an American animal lover and a camel—until I really got to know him. This pertains to many instances in my life. I think of every animal as a potential pet, but in India I found that they were thought of only as beasts of burden until they made it to a dinner plate. Camel intimacy was an oxymoron.

≡

Ramez, our camel driver, stepped up from the back, placing one foot on the spine, and straddled the burlap bundles. Clicking his tongue, he encouraged my camel to rise, first the back legs, then the front. The rein was handed to me, and I practiced steering, pulling its nose left or right. There was no Western-style neck reining on a camel; only Indian-style yanks seemed to work. Banks was on a younger camel (eight years old) and played the sheik, draping a bedsheet over his body to keep out the sun. Lurching along behind on my ten-year-old camel (whose name, Saree, I was told meant "lion"), I had a good view of his head with its many indentations, from small scalp muscles to sunken eye sockets. Barbs stuck out from each nostril where his nose had been pierced for the reins. Long lashes shaded his eyes from the light. A tuft of mane jutted out from behind his ears; he sweat there, so it glistened in the sun. Gurgles rumbled through his body, passing beneath me from front to back. His nostrils flared as he took long, smooth breaths. I found that a lumbering gait, somewhere between a walk and a trot, was most pleasant. That, I told myself, was where I'd set the cruise control.

We passed few people along the way—just a local or two on foot. We felt like kings and queens sifting through the sand with four legs beneath us.

We paused for lunch at a natural spring. The camels dipped down, front knees first, and gracefully let their hind legs fold under them. Calluses as large as their foot pads were located conveniently on their stomachs and thighs. After the camels drank their fill at the reservoir, the guides opened their bags of feed. Banks's camel, Rupee, ate sitting down. Ramez made chapatis and cut up vegetables with chili for our lunch while his brother gathered wood and camel dung for a fire. We ate within twenty minutes.

A herd of maybe seventy-five camels came to the watering hole—baby camels, adult females, and one albino male. As the young females approached, our male sputtered out sweet duets. Frothing at the mouth, his tongue gurgled out, ballooning the corners of his lips. He arched his neck, emitting a long belch, and spread his hind legs. Urine trickled out, and he slapped the pee with his tail to spread it. The albino male came up to us in a naked bid for dominance.

Journal excerpt

Camels looked like something between an ostrich and a brontosaurus. The herder milked the mothers into a brass bowl and placed it among the outstretched necks of the babies. Herds of donkeys, goats, and sheep also came to drink from the watering hole. I didn't want to think any more about the purity of our water and just hoped the tea boiled long enough. We had to periodically calm our one male (the ten-year-old) by making him lie down and tethering his front feet. The eight-year-old hadn't reached puberty yet. One camel snorted out a large caterpillar-size screwworm, which plopped on the ground and wriggled with exuberant health.

The camels Lava and Afterburner

I named our camels, of course: Lava, since they erupted from deep within; Afterburner, from the associated belch and fart; Double Up, since they caught themselves this way after they stumbled; and Stubby, for how they tripped when they encountered a stone.

We rode about four hours to a solitary Hindu temple. We would have bedded down for the evening, but the well was dry. Remains from a twenty-five-camel safari of Australians told the story of their camp; coconut shells, toilet paper scraps, and camel dung littered the barren sand. We rode another three and a half miles to a small village to find well water. I wrote by candlelight.

Camels are prehistoric. Their internal systems are crude. They constantly spit, fart, belch, and scratch. I had never before appreciated the cleanliness of horses. Once Banks and I decided to overtake the other camel during an open sandy stretch. He began running in a circle, went down on his knees, and tipped over on his side; both jockeys jumped clear to avoid being pinned beneath him. I reined in my camel but couldn't keep from laughing; the drivers enjoyed it too, though they fought to remain composed, saying, "No problem!"

My favorite parts of the day were after the ride, when Ramez and his brother made us as comfortable as possible. First they laid out our blankets. Then they fetched water and firewood and started cooking. The bags were thrown down from the camels, with their feed bags placed in front of them. There was nothing more pleasant than hearing a camel munching docilely and the sound of chapatis sizzling on a hot stove.

☰

At the last village on the eastern edge of the Thar Desert, we stopped right outside of town to water the camels from a deep well. Donkeys, cows, goats, and sheep all thronged around the same spout as we filled containers for cooking purposes.

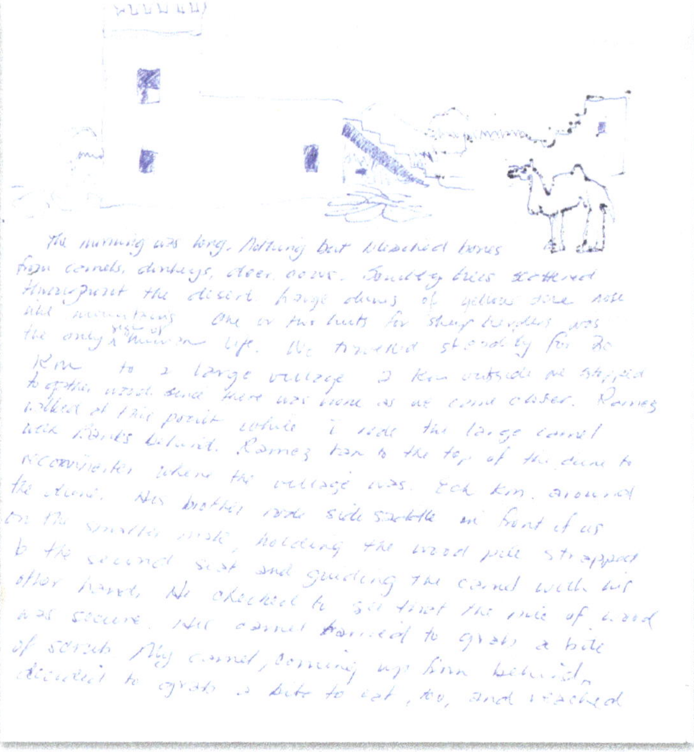

The morning was long. Nothing but bleached bones from camels, donkeys, deer, cows. Scrubby trees scattered throughout the desert. Large dunes of yellow tone rose like mountains. One or two huts for sheep herders was the only sign of human life. We traveled steadily for 20 km to a large village. 2 km outside we stopped to gather wood since there was none as we came closer. Ramez walked at this point while I rode the large camel with Banks behind. Ramez ran to the top of the dune to reconnoiter where the village was. 20 km around the dune. His brother rode side saddle in front of us on the smaller one, holding the wood pile strapped to the second seat and guiding the camel with his other hand. He checked to see that the pile of wood was secure. His camel turned to grab a bite of scrub. My camel, coming up from behind, decided to grab a bite to eat, too, and reached

Journal excerpt with drawing of a Thar Desert hut

Women balanced clay pots on their heads as they traveled to and from the well.

We rode on through the desert where only scrub brush, sand, and sky met, the blue and brown tones of the landscape swirling, inspiring carpet patterns. Plants and dunes arched upward in crescent shapes. The wind whipped across the plain, breaking up the camel jockey's melodic chant. Mysteriously, a snake appeared beside our path. Banks read the Old Testament on camelback; I read *The Lord of the Rings*. Children in villages stared, making marginal comments in Hindi. "One photo" and "Good morning" was their English.

≡

SOME THOUGHTS NOW

The Thar Desert mesa's blend of burnt umber, raw sienna, and cerulean blue still reminds me of West Texas. Camels were brought to that region in the 1860s and used by the cavalry. The terrain was too rocky for their feet, and they were turned out in the wild to survive.

I can hear the camel herder slapping dough between his hands to flatten chapatis while distant bells toll and goats bed down by their huts for the night. For forty rupees (four dollars) a night this couldn't be matched.

But how naive to ever think I could make a camel my pet. Camel intimacy with a kiss on the lips was never going to happen. I cannot even be tempted to ride a camel saddled at the zoo for short rides. They are the closest I'll ever get to imagining a ride on a prehistoric T. rex in *The Lord of the Rings*. And I could never have imagined riding eight hours on a camel, only to come to a dry well. I thought of the Three Kings of the Orient or the Queen of Sheba traveling hundreds of miles in the desert. This was normal; I was just like these travelers. I would understand my full purpose later.

THE SARI SHOP AND AN AMERICAN WOMAN

As part of his generosity, he asked me to put on his wife's wedding dress and be adorned by the women of the house.

This could have been a mirage. Our camel drivers dropped us at sunset in a town market after ten days in the Thar Desert.

Everything in the desert was still yellow or flat. We were apparently in Bikaner, which stretches like a railroad track for nearly two miles.

Our legs were disjointed from riding for so long. We wobbled, besieged by gawking children who made fun of our looks. We asked for a hotel, and bystanders pointed down the street and right or left. We asked a young man in a sari shop, who motioned for someone to get another person. A distinguished-looking man approached us. "What do you want?" he said, in precise British English. We wanted the center of town. "What do you mean by the center of town?" he said, with a creased brow.

The man, whose name was Durgar Sharma, said we were more than a mile from any hotel and invited us to have tea in his shop before we headed out in a horse cart. Then he invited us to stay in his home. We hesitated until he said he had twenty or thirty rooms. His oldest son, thirty years old, said namaste to me. I was unused to such sincere respect. We went to his home, fending off remarks like "You are a donkey" from street children. "Forgive them, for they know not what they do," I repeated to myself.

Durgar had a lovely wife, Sarala, who was holding their two-year-old son when we arrived. The couple had married when he was twenty and she was sixteen. He was now a doctor at age thirty-eight. Sarala greeted us warmly and prepared tea. The British had really shaped the customs. Banks, Durgar, and I sat in their bedroom on a large comforter, comparing Indian customs and politics to American ones.

This large Brahman family considered foreigners to be above them, like gods, even though Brahmans were of the highest Hindu caste. That's why Durgar wanted to treat us with the greatest hospitality.

As part of his generosity, he asked me to put on his wife's wedding dress and be adorned by the women of the house. I agreed, but only if it was okay with his wife. She shook her head from side to side, which meant yes, and said in beautiful English, "It is too small now."

Durgar Sharma's family with Banks and me

Banks dressed in Durgar's wedding attire to complete the family photo. Were there possible fantasies lurking in the back of Durgar's mind? Who knew? The women brought out the finest gold jewels and draped me head to toe. They delicately traced my eyelids in black and placed a red tikka on my forehead, between my eyebrows. Tikkas, which got their color from a vermillion paste, were considered the center of latent wisdom.

Sarala explained her Brahman culture when we were alone. She squatted on her ankles over a large camp stove on the floor of a room no larger than a water closet on a train. Women are respected though bound in duty to serve men continually in marriage. Marriages are arranged for daughters ages fourteen and sixteen. The woman is donated to the husband in the wedding ceremony and presents a dowry. She must wear symbols of her married state: red powder in the middle part of her hair, a red dot in the center of her forehead, ankle bracelets that jingle to let the husband know she approaches, a veil covering her head and mouth (especially when her husband is near), black kohl lines under her eyes and in the crease, red lipstick, the universal pierced nose, and many bangle bracelets.

The gracious wife spends three to six hours in the kitchen preparing lunch and dinner with tea in between. Four days a month she is considered untouchable, unhygienic, and must not associate with cooking or with men. She gets another woman to cook and is forced to hide herself away.

Because mothers have no education beyond high school, they are not considered fit teachers for their children. The children come to the father in the evenings for counsel and instruction. The mother never leaves the home.

Sarala said she had always wanted to be educated in the United States. I longed to give her the freedoms I had and wanted to set her free to come with me. It was a melancholy parting, as I felt I was abandoning her. Maybe I could have done more.

I was also trying to understand my own potential motherhood. I thought I must choose between my creative drive to be an international artist and correspondent who took up causes or to settle for the mundane life that a family represented. I did not yet know there was such beauty in having a family, as my own childhood had been extremely dysfunctional. I didn't think I could have it all. But I wanted it all.

SOME THOUGHTS NOW

After ten days on a camel, I stepped off in an unknown desert town without a plan. Next thing I knew I'd been transformed into a Brahman goddess.

My experience in Bikaner touched me on so many levels. I can't imagine coming into a barren desert town today with no knowledge of where the hotel was, if there was one at all. I didn't speak Urdu, but I wasn't concerned. Someone who spoke British English always seemed to come forward to help. All I equipped myself with was an open mind and a flexible spirit of adventure.

What stuck with me the most from Bikaner was a brewing concern for women worldwide to be free to study, marry, and have a family or, if they chose, develop careers, pursue their interests, and live without fear or domination. I never realized these things weren't possible for most women in Asia or even the United States. The generous hospitality of a Brahman family touched me personally and brought me sorrow. Indian women are property for a husband chosen by the girl's parents. That child is forevermore a servant to other needs, never developing her own. There's no way out of the trap, even if it is a gilded cage.

Sarala was one of the loveliest Indian women I've ever met. She was gracious, loving, generous, and beautiful, and she spoke excellent English, cooked, and cared for so many children. As she squatted over a small gas stove grilling chapatis, she shared her dreams with me. She wanted to travel to the United States, improve her English, and study health care to improve women's conditions in India. What an incredible heart and soul hidden away, unfulfilled, even though her home had many rooms and her family was large.

As she helped me slip into her wedding dress that no longer fit, her daughters stared at the gold jewelry they gingerly brought out. Quantity meant prosperity. Every inch of my head, hands, and feet was covered and reflected light. I asked if they could pierce my nose, but they used a clamp-on nose ring. The center red tikka brought focus to the face and established status. I felt adorned and possessed, accompanied by honor and respect, and totally embraced in their traditions. Exactly what I wanted.

Me in Sarala's wedding dress

I imagined handing my life over to a man I didn't choose but had to trust would treat me right. I had no power in this equation to keep the balance in life. I saw many men easily take advantage of young girls in the name of marriage.

Sarala's daughters stepped back to admire the American they had turned into a goddess in their own image. They giggled, pleased at what they saw. Their mother smiled quietly, and we all gathered for a family portrait; Banks had been dressed in Durgar's turban and robe. This family was honoring and including us as their own according to their Brahman beliefs that foreigners were above all as gods and goddesses.

If I hadn't stepped into Sarala's wedding dress, I wouldn't have been transformed. I wouldn't have experienced the love of her family's beliefs that keeps my heart soft for Hindus. I still align myself, though, with Mother Teresa, whom I later met in Calcutta and who fought the caste system that allows people and babies of the lowest caste to die on the streets.

≡

Naomi Shihab Nye was quoted in a 1995 edition of the *South Texas Newsletter* recounting this Asian trip. For ten years after we returned to the States, we were frequently asked to give speeches and slideshow presentations and to dress in Burmese sarongs at the Canopus Club, Kiwanis Club, San Antonio Museum of Art, McNay Art Museum, and other venues.

I think back at how the consensus in San Antonio before we left was that we were fools. When we returned, we found ourselves elevated to celebrity status. We seemed to go from street mongers to gods and goddesses.

The Sharma family prepared me to embrace my own family ten years later. They prepared me for travel to Israel twenty years later. In that parched, treeless, blinding land I recalled images of Indian women balancing pots at wells and men with long sticks riding donkeys like Jesus had, and I could embrace the humanness of Jesus for the first time as I walked the first-century Roman roads. I understood Jesus's greater love for humanity as I prayed at the rock of the Multiplication of the Loaves and Fishes by the Sea of Galilee. I no longer feared the sea of humanity I'd always tried to avoid. Jesus's love reflected in love brought bounty not scarcity, hospitality not greed, and healing. But I would never have wanted to travel

Morgan, Wright, and me, 1993

to Israel if I hadn't conquered my phobia of traveling among masses of hungry people in Nepal, India, China, and the rails of Trans-Siberia.

In Bikaner, gifts of diversity became the community. Pass it on.

SANDSTORMS AND STREET DOGS

I stepped off a camel and fell swiftly from Brahman goddess to street monger.

As we walked the streets of Bikaner I veiled myself to diminish the public abuse by children. Even when I was a teacher, I had never experienced such mockery by school kids. I tried to wrap my mind around their world. Apparently, if Indians weren't in the highest caste of Brahmans, then foreigners were below the lowest caste. What a contrast. One moment we were being treated like gods and goddesses and the next we were trashed by kids.

A pack of twenty children yelled savage words in Hindi and occasionally one in English such as "donkey." They were unsure of us and consequently ostracized us. We turned and scowled, but it made no difference. Parents observed from doorways and did nothing. Banks raised his camel stick and the children backed off a few feet but were at our heels a few seconds later, hounding us with abuse. I raised a stick and no one responded. The children poked me if they got close enough and mimicked me if I protested. I felt like a caged zoo animal. After twenty minutes of heckling we stopped in front of a Hindu shrine, stood by a wall, and faced the children. A few jumped on the wall to approach us from behind. A bold boy attempted to hit Banks, who grabbed the boy by the throat and shook him, shouting in English that he better behave. A shudder went through the crowd, and there was silence for a few moments. We weren't sure what would happen next.

Slowly the children dispersed, with sporadic shouting from a couple of hotshots. As long as we were passive about the situation, turning our backs on their behavior, they pursued us. When we showed muscle, they gave ground. They were used to "might makes right." I didn't know how to change it.

We had spent our first full moon of 1984 in the streets of Bombay. We hopped a train for several hours to spend the second full moon of the year in Pushkar, a holy city in India southwest of Bikaner. Hindus from all over India made pilgrimage to Pushkar several times a year to bathe in the holy lake and worship in the shrines. Sand dunes rose over the lake and formed scrubby hills. Trees scattered the dunes with mossy branches similar to deer antlers before rutting season.

We had seen several gurus sitting under banyans. People called them "bubbas." They invited us to talk with them at tiny shops nearby and then asked for rupees. One spoke to us in broken English of the power of sun, moon, and stones. He seemed too much a con artist to be interesting.

The first night in Pushkar Banks and I walked the streets, admiring the goat milk sweets. An open gate in a tall wall led to an interior courtyard with a lit Hindu temple rising like a miniature pyramid. I was awed by the figurines on each step, the ornate respect for so many gods.

As we were looking at the figurines, a dog latched onto my calf. I thought he was playing until pain registered as his teeth ripped through my jeans. The shock immobilized me. He twisted his head as he gripped. Banks shouted and swatted him. He released me and circled to attack from the other side. Banks moved in on him, and he retreated under some stairs.

A man across the street yelled at us to come over. He had a betel nut kiosk set up against a white-walled building. (Betel nuts, the fruit of the areca palm, are poisonous and illegal to

Site of my dog bite in Pushkar

possess in the United States but widely available in India.) He said the dog bit foreigners every night, especially if they wore jeans. I said I would kill the dog and send his head to Texas A&M University to check it for rabies. He shook his head staunchly and said, "It's against the Hindu religion to kill anything." He put "pan," a white lime paste, on my bite, pointing to the wall behind him and saying it was the same as the whitewash. Apparently it absorbed the poisons and created a scab, keeping germs on the surface to be washed away. Then he asked if he could buy my jeans. The problem was that they were on me.

A bubba saw the incident and lent us his wooden cane until the next day as protection from dog gangs. We shook it at any dog lying in the street. They knew the meaning of sticks and moved to avoid contact. Most were not aggressive.

We went back each day and observed the dog that bit me, for he lived in the street near the temple. He was ownerless and completely docile during the day, but at night he became a terror. The local people said he didn't have rabies, because a sick dog is ostracized by the others so they won't all get infected. After ten days of observation we could see that the dog didn't have rabies. I'd chosen to handle the situation in the Eastern way rather than in the Western way, fifteen days of stomach injections in the Kathmandu hospital.

I related this incident to a young American woman, Kathy, who had been traveling with us. Her father was a general in the U.S. Marine Corps and was unhappy that she was studying Buddhism while wandering through India. She tried to console me, saying that all of the dogs should be exterminated.

Banks, Wayne, me, Alvin, Karl, and Kathy in Pushkar, India

That night karma struck in an unsuspecting moment. But who believed in karma? As Kathy walked back to our hostel, a pack of dogs attacked her. She stood against a door yelling at them, but they kept lashing at her. Finally the homeowner came downstairs and thrashed the dogs away. Kathy had five to ten bites on her legs and was terrified of walking the streets again. We cleaned the wounds, but she refused to do anything else. Banks bought her a stick, and we thought more about karma while we gazed at a holy lake. The wind rippled the surface, and I imagined the fish swaying beneath.

The first-floor balcony of our hostel extended out over the lake, with sloping huts at the water's edge framing the grander sorrel sandhills beyond. Three times a year Hindu pilgrims journeyed from all over India to bathe in the lake's purifying waters and feed the fish. People chanted and turned circles in the water as it splashed on their bodies. Ashes from cremations lapped on the banks along with flowers that floated on the water's surface.

Our dormitory housed an Israeli, a West German, two Americans, and an Englishman, all in transit and introspective.

≡

Walking out on the balcony one morning I noticed a roommate fishing off the rail. He pulled a four- to five-pound fish to the surface but had no net. The fish, a large-mouthed bottom feeder, swayed slowly and flipped back into the water in the middle of being reeled up.

The second wasn't so lucky. The pole bent down to the water, and this time the fisherman flipped him tuna style over the balcony and onto the wood plank.

The West German shouted, "Don't you know this is a holy lake? People feed fish here, not kill them!"

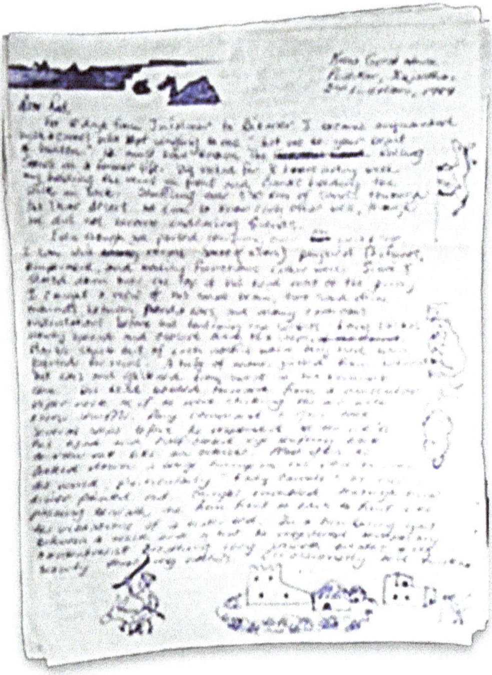

A letter I wrote from Pushkar, India

"Where is it written in scripture that I cannot fish in this lake?" the Israeli said. He turned to the Englishman lounging in the sun and asked if he had any aluminum foil, an item the locals didn't use.

The Englishman shook his head and continued lounging. Two Americans from the sandhills of Nebraska and Deadwood, South Dakota, ended their guitar playing and said, "It's your own karma."

The fish lay quietly on the boards. The fisherman moved inside to make a fire.

If a local were caught catching a fish in the holy lake he would have been publicly reproved, beaten, and paraded through the streets naked. It was unclear what would happen to a Westerner, and no one was about to tell us.

By afternoon the sky was heavy with clouds, a good time for a walk to see the coming front. The wind pressed at my tunic, snapping it like a flag at my back. People headed for their homes. I kept walking against the wind. The sandstorm hit just north of the city, the sorrel hills dissolving and swirling around the trees and temples. Hugging the base of a banyan, I watched when I could look up at all. The city was completely engulfed, lost in a flurry of sand. Donkeys and cows huddled with their backs to the wind. Sand flew off their bodies like errant spear grass. Was one person's bad karma affecting an entire city?

SOME THOUGHTS NOW

I yearn for the intimate and poignant time I spent with Brahmans, Sikhs, Israelis, Hindus, and Germans. We all interacted from our own perspectives at first but learned to bend in order to live together for a few days or weeks. This is embracing diversity even when we want to resist and hold onto our own views.

I'm not an international artist or correspondent, but I continue to strive and be fulfilled in serving the underserved as I see their needs.

In summer 2018 I flew to Honduras on an Episcopal World Mission trip to help those with the "short bone" as we tested eyes for those needing glasses. Some fifty of us nationwide lived in the small mountain villages and saw how the people there found joy in their daily life.

The irony of helping others is that it blesses me. The short bone becomes my enduring joy. The long bone increases the meaning of this odyssey as my love for humanity multiplies.

For six days we waxed ourselves in high-powered sunscreen and dipped our bodies in bug spray, an aroma that likely lingered longer than we did in the airport of San Pedro Sula, Honduras. Forty-nine of us shuffled through customs and onto the bus with fifteen large army-green duffle bags full of diapers, medicines, toothbrushes, soap, combs, towels, and children's books in Spanish.

Honduran ridgelines

We rolled with the landscape for four hours, seeing snippets of banana trees and feeling the warmth of the air and the Honduran people as we headed to Siguatepeque. A brief interlude combined our high spirits with local beer and roasted plantains as we overlooked a pristine mountain lake. Our cell phones left our family and friends in airplane mode, waiting and wondering throughout the week. What little to give up for the wealth of blessings we would give and receive from Honduran families.

A symphony of nurses, students, retired teachers, and tech experts sorted ourselves into vision teams as we slid into the second day, which happened to be Pentecost. How appropriate that the Holy Spirit interwove the material and spiritual world.

How did this translate practically? It challenged us on every level. Some of us knew no Spanish, some were quasi-fluent, and others were experts. The diversity of our age and skill sets proved to be an asset, as most young children never spoke but were curiously reading us. Brown eyes stared intently with what felt like a yearning to learn. We responded as we read their vision acuity and observed their needs. Often what we gave the most was compassion.

Pickup trucks from Café Cohorsil Coffee Company took us to one-room schools on twisty mountain gravel roads. The higher we rose the more abundant were the white coffee blooms that dotted the hillsides among the pine, banana, and eucalyptus trees.

The mode of operation was to embrace a change of plans at any moment by school administrators, even though there was a detailed schedule. If we tested a hundred students, we brought double the school gifts, knowing the testing would increase as the lineup grew. Susie, a volunteer and exceptional Spanish interpreter, encouraged good nutrition, brought seeds for gardens, and read a Dr. Seuss book out loud for students who lingered after the eye exams. We integrated into each other's cultures with total flexibility. This was our new vision for helping effectively.

Dollars contributed by the Episcopal Diocese of West Texas were greatly appreciated. The Welch Allyn Spot Vision Screener was a handheld portable device that Noreen, a nurse

Susie reading a Dr. Seuss book

volunteer, guarded with her life; it screened six-month-olds to adults with supreme accuracy. Within two seconds this oversized box camera zeroed in on the eyes and took twenty-three shots to determine a person's vision.

We tested 1,257 students, parents, and staff in four days, visiting five or six schools daily. The spot vision screener tested for amblyopia, astigmatism, hyperopia, and unequal refractive capability. The year before we had reached six hundred Hondurans in fewer schools with less accurate machines. This year more than a hundred Hondurans would receive free glasses. Vision made all the difference in a life, especially if it was corrected early.

One school especially stood out for me—the School for Special Needs, established by the International Rotary Club in

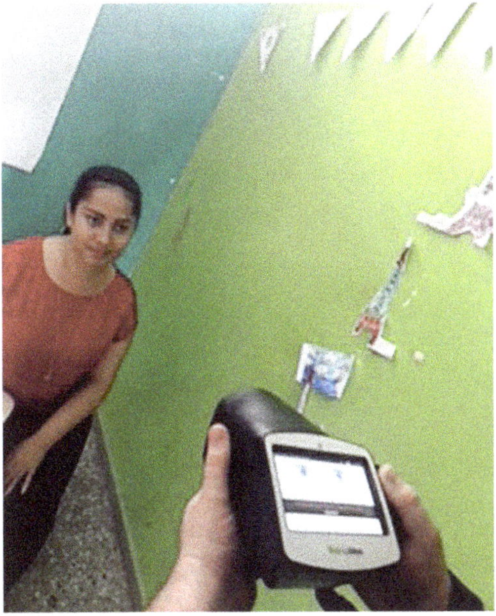

Welch Allyn Spot Vision Screener

2011. We tested fifty-eight students and teachers; twenty-two needed glasses. These children would no longer be left behind in life due to their vision.

The moment we walked into the long porch and courtyard, the students waved with what felt like the promise of hope. As we set up a dark room for testing, children lined up outside. I wrote down names one by one and directed them to the vision screener. Those who needed glasses would get them in three months.

On the sixth day I realized that many of us had bent our Western beliefs to integrate with Central American customs that were often more progressive. Recycled tires made into planters, tree stumps made into chairs, and plastic water bottle cisterns to catch water for plants were all innovative

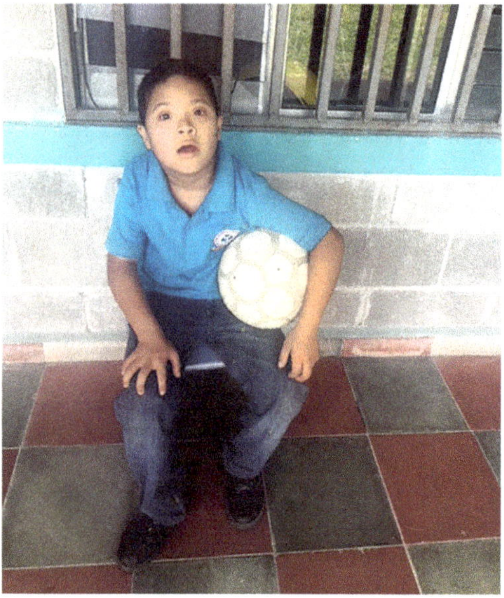

Schoolchildren in Honduras

and inspiring. Local companies and school districts worked together, such as a coffee company or toll road enterprise that paid teachers' salaries and supplies.

I've thanked many people who made this trip possible, but I want to especially thank the Diocese of West Texas. I was a recipient of a free trip; my name had been drawn from a large glass bowl the previous year at the Diocesan Council in San Marcos, Texas. I could have gone anywhere in the world where our world missions were established—Russia, Mexico, Africa, Haiti, to name a few. I chose Honduras to learn alongside my local community leaders, experts nationwide, and, most of all, the Honduran people.

CHINA

MONGOLIA
Xanadu
Ürümqi
Turpan
Gobi Desert
Beijing
CHINA
Mekong River
Xian
Himalayas
Yangtze River
Pearl River
Hong Kong

Victoria Harbor, Hong Kong

LI RIVER INK AND RURAL HOSPITAL WOMEN

We survived dog bites, bike crashes, and near abductions in Pakistan. A clear protective bubble encased us, even in China.

We were staying in the Soldiers and Sailors Home managed by the Methodist Church in Hong Kong. Rooms were spacious and clean, with old Victorian furniture and ceiling fans. Waking late, we walked out on the streets to visit a Christian Science church, the denomination of my childhood and college. We attended a service, and I saw someone I knew—Dave Scott, a physics major from my undergraduate years at Principia College in Elsah, Illinois. He said hello, and we talked about his friend from Orange County whom I used to date. Dave was in the Navy, assigned to the USS *Denver* and having R & R in Hong Kong.

We made our way to the Wan Chai district, the heart of sailors' nightlife. Neon signs were everywhere for topless bars, Suzy Wong, Crazy Horse, and the Hi Fella Seafood Restaurant. I began drawing the signs with Conté crayon, and this attracted a crowd of sailors to watch. A liquor-breathed Canadian across the street was bargaining for some velvet rugs. When he saw me, he crossed the street and wanted to buy my drawing instead. I kept working, and he kept drawing attention to himself. He said he had a brother who was a famous artist. Then he asked if I was single and said I shouldn't be sitting on a street corner in this area. A friend of his had been knifed in an alley nearby, and he and some other Canadians were going to look for the assaulters. He crossed the street and resumed bargaining for velveteen rugs.

☰

We spent the next morning in bed reading the *South China Morning Post*. The Hong Kong dollar had hit a record-breaking low of 7.04 to $1 US in international trading. We walked to the Star Ferry and boarded it for Kowloon. We saw the USS *Badger* and the USS *Blue Ridge,* flagship of the Seventh Fleet.

With the help of a Chinese-English phrase book and a basic Chinese-English dictionary, we could read a few characters on traffic signs and recognize the numbers one to ten.

The next day Banks and I walked out of a café into rush-hour traffic. Two Chinese boys on the curb rushed a third, beating him until he crumpled to the street. They kicked him until he lay still and then fled through trolley cars, taxis, buses. The owner of the café where we had just had coffee picked up the boy and took him inside. Foot traffic began to flow again, and no one thought more about it. I'd never seen anyone beaten before and wondered if this was typical.

☰

We woke at 5:30 a.m. the following day to go into China. My body had gotten weaker since Nepal, when I was exercising daily. The straps of my pack itched on my back, and I began to ache from the weight. At the Hong Kong train station, we bought tickets to Lo Wu, a border town into China.

There we would board another train for Guangzhou, which had previously been named Canton. With shifts in power in the Han Chinese government came place-name changes. People began lining up to run the gauntlet of single-person gates.

Russian submarine in Victoria Harbor

Neon signs

Some carried heavy baskets of food to sell in Guangzhou. As the gates opened, the crowd tightened. Bags, bamboo poles, and boxes were pushed along with the people. Police were patrolling, but this didn't dent the cramming through the gates as people manhandled each other for better positions. I felt myself carried off by the shifting mass, and we fled down a long stairway to get to the train, which was full. People pushed their way on anyway, some of them climbing through windows. Once we were on, we sat on our packs on the floor. The one-hour ride was anticlimactic.

On the next train, after our Lo Wu connection, the compartments were spacious and the chairs reclined. Lace curtains lined in velvet hung in the windows. There was air conditioning and music, blue hills in the distance. Rice fields tended by Chinese with water buffalo brought back memories of the silk-screened paintings in my childhood home; my grandparents had bought them on their travels fifty years earlier. Four hours later we arrived in Guangzhou.

We stayed at the Swan Hotel, an official tourist hotel, in a room with three single beds for six yuan ($2). Two giant thermos bottles filled with hot water to make green tea were brought to us. China teacups and a pot were already in the room. We dropped loose tea leaves into the cups and poured hot water. The steeped tea had a clean aroma.

☰

This area was originally built for Western import-exports when Guangzhou was the only open city in China. The streets were full of baskets of merchandise, including herbs, dry rice, live animals in cages, even a house cat. We saw tiny owls bunched together in fright. There was also an endangered species of anteater, caged alive, along with turtles, crabs, snails, and eels. We saw freshly butchered dogs. Bear claws filled one basket. It was against the law to sell bears, but if they died, the claws could be sold.

Museum artifacts

We got lost in the alleys and back streets and decided it didn't matter where we went. Any street would be fun to venture down. We entered a restaurant with caged animals outside. We could have pointed to any dog, armadillo, or weasel and been served it minutes later. We looked around for appetizing dishes the locals were eating so we'd know what we'd be getting. When the waitress came by I pointed to a dish at someone else's table. She nodded and said "soy." I said yes, thinking she'd bring me soy sauce too. Instead she brought me a large soy beer. Beansprouts with beef arrived next with sautéed vegetables and fried rice with egg and prawns. When we finished our meal I presented the front desk with my Texas driver's license, which looked like a student ID. They gave me a two-thirds discount. The meal totaled six yuan ($2), an inflated tourist price.

Bewildered Westerner

Back on the streets we were charmed by the clamor of bike bells in the night breeze. A Chinese on the street said hello and began practicing rudimentary English—how old was I, where did I live, was I married, did I have children. It was an uphill conversation.

A few days later we hopped on bus no. 3 for the main zoo in town and met a Chinese who had learned English from the radio in the early 1950s. Jumping off, we bought popsicles and went in. Two black bears were in the first enclosure. Eerily, they had the same claws I'd seen in the market. Their cage was all cement with a few rocks to climb on and a pool of water. We came to the lesser panda cage, empty and overgrown with weeds, and then the panda house. Three bears there were treated to air conditioning; there was condensation on the windows. The other cages were all cement, and the animals looked skinny and weak. We caught bus no. 6 back to the Swan Hotel and saw crowds of Chinese peering into the building, where they were not allowed. They seldom saw tourists and stared as if I were the one in the cage.

Chinese children on street

The following morning we went out for pastries and fruit. Then Banks went to purchase tickets to Wuzhou, and I sat down to draw an arched bridge. Swarms of Chinese gathered around, soon blocking my view. I felt claustrophobic but decided to make the best of it. I began drawing faces in the crowd. As I singled out a face to draw, some would begin laughing and sometimes cover their faces. Others walked away. I drew fat-cheeked children and emaciated adults. Girls wore red and white school uniforms; boys had red ties, white shirts, and white pants. An older man pointed to his profile. After I drew him he looked displeased and walked away. I hadn't actually finished and looked up into the empty space where he had been. People began to laugh. It was a wonderful way to interact without the stress of finding a common language.

Bridge on Li River

Banks returned, and we wandered past a Catholic church built around 1863 that served as a storehouse but opened at set hours for worship. We walked into a roadside café to eat. We pointed to what we thought was beef and green peppers over rice. When it came the man said it was "er er" and pointed to his stomach. Cow, pig, buffalo, dog, cat, duck, rat? No, it was a goose's stomach, extremely expensive (nine yuan, more than $3).

≡

Our schedule for the next few days included a twenty-hour boat ride up the Pearl River to Guangzhou, a ten-hour bus ride to Yangzhou, nine days in Yangzhou, and a twelve-hour boat ride up the Li River to Guilin.

≡

Over the following six weeks, I painted each new bend in the Li River as we traveled upstream toward Guilin, a beautiful, prosperous tourist town. After six bends I stopped painting and took in the scenery with my eyes. The mountains rose a thousand feet perpendicular to the river. Receding mountains echoed each other's shapes in shades of light blue. The black ink and round brush seemed designed to capture the many tones of riverbank, foliage, and nearby mountains. We pressed slowly upstream, the swift current against us.

Three punting bamboo boats pulled up alongside us, the fishermen displaying their catch. Birds like pelicans were tethered to the reeds with neck rings so they would dive down, catch fish, and come up but not swallow them. We passed villages of Chinese who waved at us as they were cleaning a side of pork and bathing themselves in that same water. Water buffalo swam near our ferry while children cast stones at them from shore. Ferries passed us quickly going downstream to Yangzhou. Tourists heading that direction paid double because of the speed.

We had noodle soup with spring onions for breakfast. Lunch was fresh fish from the boats braised in sweet-and-sour sauce along with some unidentifiable vegetables.

We waited at a popular tourist hotel while a random Chinese "friend" bought us bus tickets so we could pay him a little extra in tourist money. There were two types of currency—clean for tourists and dirty for locals. Only tourist money could be

Li River

exchanged in diplomatic stores for luxury goods. Most local people never laid hands on the clean currency.

Four large tourist buses pulled up in front of the hotel. The passengers were in their mid-thirties to fifties and all overweight. The British men sat in the aisle, the women by the windows. As they came down the steps, the men puzzled over what to do with their half-full beers. They tried giving them to the Chinese guides, who said they could take them to their rooms. The women passed us with a frown or a smile of approval at our backpacks, depending on whether they thought us adventuresome or a slur on genuine tourism. They mostly had packaged gifts in hand, camera bags on their shoulders, and rolling suitcases, as if they were going on safari.

When we got to our $3 hotel in Guilin on the Li River we were told the house was full. Nine of us sat in protest in the lobby; there was nowhere else to go. Sometimes the staff would turn down travelers because they were paid a flat rate whether they cleaned one bedroom or two hundred. We waited twenty minutes and approached the desk again. They said a room was available on the third floor. There were three beds to a room and nine of us waiting for three rooms, including two lesbians and three married couples; someone would have to split up. No one wanted to, so Banks and I did. I went with an American couple and he with the Canadian and Swiss.

≡

Most of our information came from talking to travelers, as printed information was scarce. We became excellent judges of character because our well-being depended on it. We wondered if Margaret Thatcher had won the election the week before. In Guilin women on the streets approached us to "change money." These were the first signs of prostitution. Free enterprise was more open here. The farms were run by families rather than communes.

The last night in Yangzhou I painted the mountains while Banks swam in the river below. An old woman with no front teeth came up to me several times to say hello. Her four-year-old grandson gave me jasmine flowers from the trees nearby. I gave him a small Texas flag, which delighted him, although I felt stupidly patriotic. The grandmother began describing the painting to me. If she liked something she gave me a thumbs-up. She pointed to the mountains, comparing them to cat ears. Then she asked, "Where is your husband?" When Banks returned, she invited us to her home, which was one room with a loft. On the walls were posters showing Chinese life and one of Mao on a red stallion. She had pictures of herself and her husband during the Revolution. Her eyes sparkled. She switched on a portable TV, which showed static. I could hear an English class repeating words from a nearby building. She pointed to me and made it clear by gestures that she had heard me speak to the class the night before about my bicycle crash. Her thumbs flashed up again, and we both smiled. Banks drew a map of the world, locating the United States, Texas, and China. He drew the flags for each, and the woman nodded in understanding when we gave her our state flag. When we got ready to leave she seemed saddened and heartened at the same time. She came into the street and grabbed my hand, squeezing it hard. We walked down the block hand in hand and parted at the corner.

We walked into an open-air basketball court three-quarters the size of a regular court. Chinese players averaged about five feet, three inches, with some a little taller. The teams were easy with each other, as a quick toss and basket would be made by one and then the other. They never had more than two or three setups and lacked the mastery that comes from playing the sport on the streets from a young age, but they exhibited great enthusiasm.

We wandered into the Guilin market and found quantities of dried food pressed flat—starfish, lizards, and mushrooms. There were maybe twenty herbs for medicinal purposes as well as live foods—cages of pigeons, owls, anteaters, cats, turtles, snakes, rabbits—then more baskets of bear paws with claws, fur, and pads. Fresh-butchered meat consisted of chicken, duck, goose, cow, fish, and dog.

Down a side street we stopped inside a small café filled with local Chinese. Everyone seemed to be eating one of two dishes. We pointed to the chicken leg and spinach. The waitress nodded and first brought us Chinese pilsner. Everyone was drinking beer and staring at us. Games began at the tables, betting with the hands making numbers. As people guessed right or wrong, shouting followed. The noise level rose as more began playing. Several tried to talk to us in Cantonese. We said "America," which they didn't understand. "U.S." did not compute either, and we felt better for being off the beaten track. Our food came in ample portions, and we tucked in heartily with chopsticks. We heard more laughter as people watched. One bold Chinese came up to show us how to hold the chopsticks. Apparently they were more distressed by Banks's approach than mine. The bowl was lifted to his mouth, and he was encouraged to shovel it in. He nodded and did, which made everyone happy. The meal cost one and a half yuan (seventy cents) and was nutritious and tasty.

Temple of Heaven

We ambled down the street past a six-hundred-year-old tower five stories high housing historic artifacts, imported items such as cuckoo clocks and ornate glass lamps from dynasties long ago.

We were well into June. As I waited an hour and a half in the north train station for the train to Chengdu, I thought back on a bicycle trip through rice paddies that had started out harmlessly. Banks and I had rented bicycles in Yangzhou for two yuan each. Trucks honked as they passed us in the city streets. Two bicycles headed to the city market passed, each with a side of pork from fresh-slaughtered pigs. Other Chinese balanced vegetables in baskets on either end a bamboo pole as if they were carrying large scales. Grander trucks passed us, more bicycles and walkers going the other direction. The cool morning breeze aired my shirt, brushed my hair. Lush rice paddies swayed on either side. Some were swamped from the fast-flowing streams nearby. Large clumps of dung were piled in neat rows. Perpendicular mountains were reflected in the water. The frogs were louder than the truck horns, and soon they were all we heard. Trees shaded the road, splitting sunbeams for me to pass through. Miniature Chinese walls separated rice fields from the mountains. Water buffalo stretched their muscles under yokes as farmers' guttural shouts steered them.

Approaching a river crossing, I saw several buffalo swimming along the banks. A ferryman loaded his passengers and bicycles and poled the wooden canoe left side and right. A buffalo got herded into the water, held by a rope attached to its nostril and hooked around his head, submerging its whole face at times. As the boat neared the far shore the buffalo was sandwiched between boat and shore. The owner hopped onshore and led it along the bank behind the boat. The passengers leaped out with their baskets. I hoisted my Pigeon Flyer bicycle from the canoe, and we rode down dirt roads through paddies. Dikes crossed the path at intervals, forcing me to walk my bike across, straddling flat stones. The rice grew knee-high, a haven for frogs and turtles. No wonder so many were for sale in the markets. Stone pathways led right and left past one-room houses with children playing in the doorways. Mountains met rice paddies with an interval of forested land.

Separating wheat from chaff

I sat down to paint at the edge of the path. Children gathered around me, chattering in Chinese. An older woman walking by dispersed them to the fields with a scolding. Banks explored and returned to sit in the shade to read. Children came by again. I gave them some pens and decided not to corrupt them with rubber bands and Texas flags. The sun was high in the sky, a new slant on the day. We returned to the ferry, and once we were across the ferryman asked for eight yuan. He was a government employee, making a little on the side. We approved the capitalist venture and paid him. There it was a big deal, but I wouldn't think anything of giving a tip in the United States.

We hopped on our bikes again, clearing the top of a loose gravel hill. My bike naturally gained momentum. As I pressed back on my pedals to slow, the tires skidded out from under me. I skated down the hill on the palms of my hands through loose gravel. At the bottom I lay still and went into shock. My palms had been grated by rocks, so they bled and remained numb. We couldn't figure out how to get back to town four miles away. A Chinese boy working in the fields half a mile away saw us and came running over. He bent the bike back into shape and hopped on. I mounted behind him but couldn't use my hands to hold on. Using my arms, instead I kept my seat while he peddled in front. When we reached the city he waved goodbye and we gave him a John Lennon T-shirt. He would walk back home.

We entered a hospital around 6 p.m., just as it was closing. Women doctors were heading toward the door when they noticed us. They inspected my wounds and did a painfully thorough cleansing to remove all the gravel from my hands. One doctor cleaned my hands while the other smoked, tipping her ashes out an open window over some surgical masks that were drying. We were grateful nonetheless and paid them nine yuan for the inspection and cleansing.

SOME THOUGHTS NOW

When I sat down on a street corner in Chengdu to draw an arched bridge, it seemed like an ordinary thing to do. Why

Chinese Buddha

would people block your view when they saw you drawing a landscape? That was a foreign concept to me, and it was a foreign concept to the Chinese for someone to draw on a street corner. My solution was to begin a group portrait of the group who had formed in front of me. When they recognized their faces they shrieked and laughed but stayed. It was a wonderful interaction. I realized that routines I take for granted are very odd to the Chinese. The ordinary becomes extraordinary, and perceptions are questioned in a friendly way.

What took me down the path of giving and receiving grace? I survived dog bites, bike crashes, even a near abduction in Pakistan, and never fully understood the dangers as I seemed to have a bubble encasing me. The Chinese buddha was not affected by the dragon looming over his shoulder. Nor am I.

I look at my right palm, and I can still see the tiniest grain of sand embedded in it. As I skid through many journeys in life, this grain reminds me that we're all imprinted with flesh stories.

YANGTZE GORGE, FIRSTBORN GIRL, AND TERRACOTTA UNDERGROUND

Special rice was thrown into the river for fish so they wouldn't eat Qu Yuang's body. Dragon boats raced to find the dead poet and created surface movement to help raise it.

In July 1983 we left Guilin for a seventeen-hour train ride to Xinjiang, where we'd switch to a twenty-four-hour ride to Chengdu, a prominent town in south-central China that displayed a grand statue of Mao towering over a boulevard. We barely found spots on the floor, using our packs for seats. Once again Chinese flooded onto the train through doorways and windows. Some people lay on the floor in the aisle. The actual seats were straight-backed boards with a thin layer of padding. Knees touched elbows and elbows pushed shoulders as people crammed together for seventeen hours. The person by the window controlled the air. Chinese seem to chill easily and kept the windows mostly shut. I felt stifled and claustrophobic. I dozed until reflex jerked my nodding head awake. Around 2 p.m. a stone came flying through a window, shattering glass over passengers one seat ahead of us. People seemed unconcerned. I drifted into a dazed noncommunicative state. A French girl spoke fluent Mandarin with those around her; apparently she'd spent two years in Taiwan learning it. By the end of seventeen hours I was exhausted.

The pack wore heavily on me as I carried it to the train station. An attendant ushered us into a secluded room with Chinese rugs and high-backed chairs. I collapsed into one. As this was a closed town, we weren't supposed to venture far and were monitored during our stay. Banks was allowed to buy food while I stayed with our packs. He returned an hour later with pastries and bananas. A Chinese railroad worker helped him while practicing his self-taught English and gave him a coupon to use. He said he made thirty-seven yuan a month. He asked Banks if he'd heard of infanticide. In this city, first-born girls were killed. The parents needed boys to carry on the family property, and because the government allowed only one child per family, it must be male. If a family did have a girl, the husband could divorce the wife. Parents with two children had their wages cut in half and their children weren't allowed to attend the best schools.

We boarded a train that was not too crowded and acquired hard berths. For twenty-six yuan we skirted the crowd and found peace. The ride was cool, the accommodations spacious and pleasant. As the sun set, we had a bed and constant locomotion to relax us. The water reflecting in rice paddies looked like shiny silkworm threads.

A Chinese who spoke good English invited us to dinner. He explained some of the differences between the English and Chinese languages. You couldn't say "two mountains" or "three buses" in Chinese; there was a separate word for these. He also showed us hand gestures for numbers.

Because we had berths, we were among higher-class Chinese. We met a man who had been working in a factory in Kunming for twenty years, with a family in Shanghai he was permitted to see once a year. The government assigned him to Kunming because that's where workers were needed. He waited on me, getting hot water for my tea, and changed seats with me when the sun was too bright on my side.

≡

I sketched my surroundings. There were triple bunk beds, two pullout seats beneath windows, two tables with our teacups, and a Chinese woman eating by a window. I began drawing a man nearby eating with chopsticks. He decided to draw me too and did so in ink on the palm of his hand. We showed each other our drawings and laughed. The train stopped for a food break. A salesperson gestured the price with his hands. We bought fermented beans in soy sauce and Rice Krispies for dessert.

Demon statues, Divine Light Monastery

Man eating rice

≡

Reflections floated across the surface of a jar of weak yellow tea on the counter by the window. They curved around the jar, seeming to stir the tea in a swirl. Objects nearer the train moved around faster than those farther away. The landscape's greens and reds blurred in the jar's reflection. The scenery flowed by in it, sometimes with lines, other times blank sky. Through the tea I could read how fast the train was going, what we passed, how close or far it was from the train. I was learning to read the leaves too.

We slept for two full days in Chengdu, waking to lounge, drink tea, and read the *China Daily*. Around noon we went out to try a couple of dishes some Chinese friends had recommended. At one restaurant we found a crowd of people buying a special kind of rice wrapped in leaves for a festival the next day commemorating the poet Qu Yuang, a loyal supporter of the Shu during the period of the Warring States (475–221 BCE). Persecuted by colleagues and forced into exile, he wrote poems about his beloved state. On the fifth day of the fifth lunar month he drowned himself, tying a large rock to his chest and jumping into a swift-flowing river. The Chinese celebrate this date each year. Special rice is thrown into the river so the fish won't eat the poet's body. Dragon boats race to find the body and create surface movement to help raise it.

The previous day we had gone to the Divine Light Monastery just north of Chengdu. Baskets, drinks, fans, and assorted rice dishes were hawked on the road to the monastery. High-ceilinged rooms housed statues of people and Buddhas. One was filled with ten-foot statues of demonic men. I walked down an avenue of contorted faces, all of the figures starting above eye level. I drew pictures in my journal to capture the facial expressions.

The first two nights in Chengdu we went out with some Chinese university students who approached us on the street to practice their English. I tried to learn Chinese words for things we passed: bicycle, tree, sidewalk, street. We went to a teahouse and spent time with the old men there drinking tea and telling stories. An older English teacher and two Chinese girls joined us. One was a public hygienist, the other a grocer. They explained that they had no choice of career. If their families were grocers, they would be grocers. They had American friends and occasionally got *Vogue* magazine in the mail to see what the United Sates was like. They both wanted to be interpreters so they could travel around China and meet tourists. At present no one in China traveled much due to the lack of vacations and holidays. The English teacher was interested in politics. He asked if the Kennedy assassination had been resolved and wanted to know who shot Reagan. He referred to ten years during the Cultural Revolution when people stayed indoors for fear of being shot. They walked us to our hotel, and I gave them George Eliot's *Middlemarch*. They had read *Jane Eyre*, so they were ready for English society in the nineteenth century.

Banks and I found a foreign-language bookstore and bought some Chinese literature, including *The Construction of the People's Republic of China*, *The True Story of Ah Q* by Lu Xun, *Pilgrimage to the West*, *Flowers in the Mirror*, *Lu Xun's Selected Poems*, and *Selected Poems of Bai Juyi.*

I drew the front of Mao Tse-tung's statue on Chengdu Boulevard. His arms extended outward over the broad boulevard. I added the billboard behind him with the words "Plan your family for a better future" and a woman doctor pointing at a newly married couple, all smiles. She held an open book in her other hand.

I found posters of Marx, Engels, and Stalin, as well as Mao on a fiery red stallion. As I walked out of the bookstore, a man on a bicycle stopped to say hello. A doctor, he invited me to his clinic where he did acupuncture and massages and worked with stroke victims and patients with color blindness and

Statue of Mao Tse-tung

rheumatism. He showed me pictures of American friends and offered to give me a massage; I declined, saying I'd like to see acupuncture performed first.

At noon we entered the streetside clinic through a white cloth doorway with a large red cross in the center. Patients with acupuncture needles in their shoulders and backs sat quietly and smiled at us. Wu, the doctor, rode up on his bike again, explaining that he also managed a clinic behind a hotel. He stuck more needles in patients. One man came every day to be treated for rheumatism; the needle marks in his arm were proof. Wu asked again if I wanted an acupressure massage, and this time Banks said yes for me. I climbed onto a waist-high table with a mat that stretched full length. He began with the back of my neck, pressing either side of center. He rubbed and felt for a particular spot and applied finger pressure that sent energy straight to the center of my skull. I felt equal pleasure and pain as pressure was applied. When his fingers relaxed, so did my body, until he found another pressure point. Then he'd hone in on me like a worker bee to a hive. He rapped on my skull. I felt the heaviness of his touch and the pleasure that came when he released it. He asked what I was feeling and where. The jugular vein in my neck began feeling the pressure; my head got numb and started tingling. Blood rushed to my head again, and I felt relieved and relaxed. Pounding palms penetrated my back. Fingertips inched up my back like a lazy worm. At the shoulder blades he began rubbing again. I felt a temporary pain through to my breasts as he popped a tender bone. On my stomach I became a washboard under hands that flattened and brushed up my legs again and again to the hip. Fingers probed and found what they were looking for. He popped an ankle bone, which saturated my foot with pleasurable pain. The release brought the most pleasure. On my back again he rubbed and soothed me, treating my breasts as he would any other part of my body. Always when the pressure released, there was a rush of relaxing pleasure. Hands worked up my legs again, finding points to press. Halfway up my calf, a finger dug into the muscle and numbed my lower leg and toes. The last two toes in particular moved slightly under the pressure. This doctor was an excellent marksman, hitting a bullseye with every pressure point.

A chart on the wall showed 365 pressure points in the body along twelve vertical channels. I dreaded his having to press each one and realized that he was doing exactly that. He gently massaged my entire body and asked how I felt. I couldn't move; I was so relaxed and glad it was over in a slow thirty minutes. I felt like a thoroughly poked dough boy. We talked a while as I lay there recovering. He asked if we would like to see his other clinic, and we sauntered over in the cool breeze. I drank herb tea and saw a photograph on the wall of Wu's grandfather and Mao. The grandfather was Mao's doctor.

Wu began diagnosing Banks by feeling his pulse. Banks's heart, bladder, intestine, and lungs were all strong. His kidney was questionable. He had a dry throat and a slight fever. Wu took a needle-nosed probe attached to a battery pack Banks held in his hand and touched different parts of Banks's ear to diagnose his organs again. (If a beep stayed high and constant it was a sign that a particular organ was weak or disordered.) He diagnosed me in the same manner. He said my menstrual cycle was in disorder. I had a hot breath from the air, but the organs were otherwise strong. Through the beeper he said he could also tell what parts of my female organs were the most sensitive. I laughed at this and wanted to know, of course, but he wasn't able to translate names of body parts.

He prescribed a fragrant medicine for the temples in the heat of the day and herbs to take with tea for our dry throats. Then he took us to an inexpensive, delicious restaurant where we had pork and green vegetables over rice for $1. He took us to the train station and bought tickets for us at the local rate. Tourists paid 70 percent more unless they could prove they were students. Ten yuan bought us hard berths on a twelve-hour ride to Chongqing.

Wu met our needs in a variety of ways; for him, it was a diversion. As we walked the streets this young bachelor taught me about what counted as beauty in a Chinese woman. She must be well proportioned and at least five feet, six inches, with large facial features but none of them dominant. A yellow cast in some peasant women was considered undesirable.

I learned a lot about China in a short time from Wu. He joked with us in English and had a girlfriend with whom he spoke English. We exchanged addresses and promised to write. Reflecting back several weeks later, I noted that the twelve-hour train ride from Chengdu to Chongqing was actually pleasant. There weren't more people than seats, and we sat across from older people as eager to learn English as we were to learn Chinese. Banks would go down a row in a phrase book, pick a character, and say the English word next to it. The passengers practiced the English word and gave us the Chinese. Others gathered in the aisle, and soon it was "Where are you from?" and "What is your job?"

Banks came back from washing his face and set the toothpaste down beside his toothbrush. One man stretched curiously for a closer look at Colgate.

Meanwhile I walked the narrow hallway to open a hobbit-like bathroom door. The sound of the wheels clicking over rails came through a hole in the floor, along with such air as circulates. The pee went straight onto the tracks if a person kept steady. Not many people had been steady, and the two-foot-wide compartment was stagnant with the smell of urine. I squatted feet apart on a raised platform, one hand on a grip at eye level. I took great care not to miss the hole, given the bounces and jiggles.

On the street, babies waddled with split pants, liberating them from diapers. The entire street was both bathroom and playground. Pigtails flagged the back of old women's heads. Dwarfed feet on wooden stilt shoes walked slowly, gracefully, in dainty strides. Radio-taught English speakers descended on us, devouring the elusive "correct" pronunciation. Bing Gao popsicles splotched the sidewalk with drips. Pale pulpy fat clung to the skulls of hog heads in the open-air slaughterhouse. Stubby hairs poked out like played-out brushes. People walked through vegetable and meat markets carrying live chickens by their wings or ducks by their feet. Sections of pork hung on strings in people's hands swayed from side to side. Women held their babies up to see the foreigners. Some piped hello; others looked away. Quick beeps sent people scurrying to the side of the road to make way for a 1950 Russian Biaza car with its curtains drawn. A pushcart of cigarettes was overturned and a squabble ensued. A crowd gathered to watch two women work it out through screaming.

We didn't waste any time purchasing and boarded a boat for a four-day trip through the Yangtze River from Chongqing to Yichang. We passed three major gorges three thousand feet high jutting vertically from the river. The mountains were giant ribs of a beached whale, the Yangtze its bloody ooze. A future dam had been proposed that would flood the gorges, villages, and farmland while raising the river level.

Along with twenty-two others, we had fourth-class bunks in a cabin the width of the boat with a door at each end. Our bunk was nearest to the door, so we had the most breeze and the grandest view. A Swiss couple and an American couple were nearest us.

As we explored the boat we stepped over fifth-class passengers lying in hallways. Women held babies to their breasts to nurse; men bent over their baggage, exhausted; old men stretched feeble limbs on bamboo mats. One wore a towel around his head. He leafed through my sketchbook; I pointed to him and to a blank page. His face lit up with delight, accenting the wrinkles. He took off his towel, and I motioned it back on. By this time the crowd extended as far as the deck and people were blocking my only fluorescent light. Someone noticed and pushed people aside. An hour later I'd finished. The man seemed proud of himself and the drawing. I showed them more sketches, and our parting smiles were kind.

As I drew the gorges outside my window, a Chinese man watched over my shoulder, then showed me his own oil miniatures of portraits. I was impressed. Another artist came up

Yangtze River gorge

Chinese artist's portrait of me

with his book. We exchanged addresses and were glad to meet. One asked me to draw him on a page of his book. I did a quick pencil portrait. I asked both to draw me in mine and thought one drawing exceptionally nice.

The following day the gorges were moody. The wind blew hard, and the scenery changed rapidly. I sneaked up to second class (there is no first; people are "equal" in China) to be at the front of the boat and take in the panoramic view. A woman from Rhode Island began drawing too, saying she had been encouraged by seeing me draw. We went into the hallway to draw people. I chose a man sleeping over a rice bag. A crowd formed to watch. He began to tip and then fell completely on the floor. The crowd began to laugh as he got up and walked away, no doubt feeling he had lost face.

三

We arrived in Yichang around 5 p.m. At the train station I drew a billboard that covered a twenty-foot wall with the words "Realization toward Modernization." Four faces represented peasants, workers, soldiers, and scientists. Mushroom clouds in the background, rockets ready to launch, and in the sky, grain silos, trains, parading masses holding red flags, their right arms raised. No minority was left out at the bottom of the billboard, and all were identified by color and style of dress. There definitely seemed to be a class system, with minorities at the bottom. The boat offered second and third class and twenty-four-person cabins in fourth. Fifth was in the hallway.

In Yichang we were asked if we were students. We replied yes, but they wouldn't give us the discount. We had to be students in China. There was a 75 percent surcharge for tourists.

From about 10 p.m. to 3 a.m. we rode hard straight-backed seats to Luoyang in the northwest province. Two children fell asleep in their parents' arms across from us. A six-year-old

Propaganda billboard near Luoyang

got too heavy for one mother, and she laid a mat on the floor for him. His head stretched into the aisle, so she had to watch constantly that no one stepped on him. People cleared their throats and spat on the floor. A man swept cigarette butts, empty food boxes, popsicle sticks, and other waste right into the child's hair. The mother brushed it out. Coal soot clung to our clothes, arms, and faces. Every part of my body wanted to find a new position; there wasn't one. I shifted my weight, read to occupy my mind, walked to the scalding samovar for hot water for tea. The only real pleasure was knowing that the ride would end in a few hours.

At 3 a.m. we came to a poor unnamed town to connect with the 9:30 a.m. train that would take us, in ten hours, to

Luoyang. No English-speaking Chinese invited us to a VIP room, as had happened in other closed towns on our route. Beggar lads, bare chested and dirty, stretched out on the station floor. The ticket counter personnel wouldn't accept our driver's licenses as student IDs, so we paid fourteen yuan per ticket instead of four; we hardly cared and cleaned a spot of sidewalk to sit on. I dozed until dawn. Many peasants woke and began sorting out the day. It was a relief to be on a hard seat on the train to Luoyang. When we arrived, we took a bus from the train station to an air-conditioned hotel in a daze. The hotel, at five yuan a person, had starched white sheets and hot showers, which I thoroughly indulged in. Banks and I slept an entire day.

While in Luoyang, we wanted to catch bus no. 3 to the Longmen grottos. These famous fifteen-foot statues were outside and inside of caves, though the heads had disappeared or were destroyed long ago by theft or tribal wars. In the 1930s French Jesuit priest, mystic, and scientist Pierre Teilhard de Chardin had discovered the Peking skull, the oldest human remains found thus far, in these caves.

When bus no. 3 came by, it was full. We decided to take another bus to the terminal and walked fifteen minutes to a stop. The bus pulled up empty and stopped in front of a crowd. Feral pushing and shoving were how one got inside. Old people, mothers with children—no one was spared. We decided to walk to the terminal. There a man took our money, and we were the only ones to board. It was nice to be on the inside looking out at the first stop. The doors swung open, and an immediate push crammed the people in front so much that some stuck in the passageway and squirmed their way free. A flood of passengers and baggage filled every possible space. We sat by open windows to escape the stale air. The bus began to move, honking at every donkey cart, shit wagon, and smaller truck in its path. My ears went numb in the half-hour ride.

The Longmen grottos were magnificent but also disappointing. Nearly all of the statues' faces were gone. A Chinese said it was in this century that the Chinese made off with them to sell to tourists. It appeared that European museums preferred the heads of famous statues. China kept the tails.

We climbed back on bus no. 3 for a sardine ride home and made our way to the Luoyang station to get local tickets to Xian. We approached with our driver's licenses and twenty yuan. Our pictures were questioned. Banks showed the other local tickets we'd bought. The agent accepted this and processed us for Xian at eight yuan each. The train left at 10 p.m. and arrived at 4 a.m. We took bus no. 6 out to White Horse Temple, the first Buddhist temple in China. The Tang dynasty Buddhas, who were thin, were transported here by white horses, hence its name. The Buddhas bore red tikkas on their heads, an Indian influence. The grounds were serene and tranquil. A sense of grace returned to my limbs, my person, if I could only hold onto it boarding a crowded bus.

It felt as if we had been in Xian for several days, though we had arrived in the early hours of the morning. We familiarized ourselves with the city layout, explored a little, and called a friend in San Antonio. The city was a grid. North, south, east, and west gateways made streets perpendicular and parallel. We saw the north gate's tower, which signaled time with a two-tone bell, as well as the tower where drums were beaten for the closing of the gates at night. The great mosque next to it was elegant with its stone wall and furniture. The Muslims wore white snug-fitting caps. There were fifty thousand of them in this city of 1.5 million Chinese. The mosque was built in the Silk Route days when many Muslims traveled. We ate nearby, enjoying a dish of noodles, ground beef, and green onions.

The day before we had toured the Shaanxi province museum for several hours with two bilingual guides who practiced English by relaying Chinese history. In the museum I did

Little Wild Goose pagoda near Xian

sketches of bronzes, ceramics, and stone carvings of dynasties that had once controlled Xian. There had been eleven. From there we walked to the Little Wild Goose pagoda from the Big Wild Goose pagoda, a distance of seven miles. These were built in the Tang dynasty, in 648 BCE, to house more than six hundred volumes of Buddhist scriptures brought from India and translated into Chinese by Xuanzang.

三

The local bus to the Terracotta Army stopped at a side street by our hotel, which we discovered after hopping on a tourist bus offering an hour at the vaults for three yuan a person. We jumped off and caught the local behind us for just one yuan!

Traveling to the site, we met an English-speaking Chinese and his friend and spent the day together exchanging cultural history for English lessons.

Terracotta soldiers

The first wing of the site was airplane-hangar size and had the best-preserved soldiers of assorted ranks. Apparently each was a replica of a real contemporary soldier. Tourists looked down on hundreds of them and dozens of horses lined up in rows. Toward the end of the vault we saw sections that were only partway excavated. Heads, arms, and shoulders lay partially exposed; it was thrilling to imagine what was still under the earth. Each soldier was distinct in how he wore his hair, tilted his head, or slanted his body. All had uniforms and characteristic stances reflecting their individuality, which seemed contradictory to me in the current Chinese culture. Thumbs turned out, hands cupped under, arms otherwise stiff. They all seemed intelligent and alert. I sketched an archer, a horse, and the general layout of the vault and tried to imagine the emperor Qin Shi Huang, who for thirty-six years forced thousands of peasants to make these sculptures to preserve their lord. Actually, they preserved themselves. The vivid images of the dress, size, and general appearance of these Chinese from 221 BCE was startling.

三

From there we traveled some six miles by bus to hot springs at Li Shan (Li is "black" and Shan is "mountain"). Here Chiang Kai-shek was prevented by two of his generals from escaping the Communist party in December 1936, and here the emperor Qin kept his favorite concubine, who sang, danced, and painted.

We ate lunch in the town at the foot of Li Shan. The local dishes were a steamed meat dumpling dipped in soy sauce and a chicken noodle soup, filling and mild-flavored. We walked upward, passing photographers and popsicle and hot drink vendors. People called to us from under umbrellas and dangled things at us. A third of the way up the mountain they fell away. The walk wound easily up to a quaint monastery that served tea with Kamadeva, the male god of anything a person supposedly desires. About twenty minutes from the summit I stopped to draw the city below and the cliff-hung monastery. We meandered down past a steeply shingled fifteen-foot waterfall among jagged pink and rust-colored rocks.

On reaching the lower, rolling hills we came upon some peasants who made their homes in hillside caves. They invited us to their homes for tea. In one we found a coffin ready for the mistress of the family when she died. There were seven in the family, plus five children, all older than the one-per-family policy instituted a year before. Several families lived together communally. Each farmed its five acres, cared for its cow and a few chickens. The main crop was wheat. They separated the chaff with a large rolling stone column pulled by a cow. They also spread wheat across the road and let buses run over it. Then the farmer swept it back into a pile for the buses to run over again. Later in the day he tossed it in the air and let the wind blow away the chaff. Farmers worked until sunset, around 7:30 p.m. We returned to Xian exhausted and fulfilled.

One morning we spent time writing to parents, aunts, and a friend. Around noon we took a bus to the Banpo museum, which described a Neolithic people sedentary in nature and matrilineal in structure. Land passed from mother to daughter. Women controlled agriculture; hunting was secondary. Their pottery employed stylized deer, fish, and so on; they even had pottery steamers for vegetables. They first lived in round clay huts with a moat to separate clans and then developed the square houses with pitched roofs we know today. They domesticated dogs and pigs. Infant mortality was high; babies were buried in earthen jars. The people were orderly and took care of their possessions, it seemed. I was moved by this knowledge of an early matriarchal society. What happened to destroy it?

Afterward we went to the zoo, which depressed me as the animals were thin. The wild dogs had mange and no water. The condors couldn't stretch their wings without batting them against the cage. They were losing their feathers and huddled in their shadows. It looked like slow death. We saw an eagle owl, a bird formerly abundant in China until they were all eaten, with huge yellow eyes and a panting beak. A solitary zebra kept biting its shoulder. Two giraffes fought over food, the larger dominating the smaller. The elephant had a big bulge in its side. One Chinese worker threw tomatoes to the monkeys with an ill grace, as if thinking, "I should be eating you rather than feeding you." The camels' humps were slumping and matted. Ostriches came so close to the fence that the Chinese got to pluck their feathers. "In Guangzhou they'd be in someone's stew," Banks said.

We were out on the streets at 8:30 a.m. the next day to get tickets for Turpan, a Uighur ethnic border city in the Gobi Desert of northwestern China. The ticket counters directed us back and forth until we found the right kiosk, which was closed. A man sprayed the slab of cement we stood on with a hose and four women swept the water away. Chinese standing in line had to scatter as he moved. Banks and I decided to have breakfast. We returned to find the team still hard at work, although the area they were cleaning was ten feet square. We realized why China had no unemployed. Efficient or not, everyone does something. When they finished, the counter opened and we were given a written note and directed around the corner of the building.

We went to that spot and handed the paper to a person we guessed might be in charge. He took us to another building, where we sat for forty minutes watching Chinese work at desks. Ultimately they paid attention to us, and we showed them the train number we needed for the next day. The woman checked the schedule and pointed to some English words with Chinese next to them: "today," "morning," "noon," "night." We pointed to "tomorrow" and "hard berth." They gave us two slips of paper and motioned for us to go to another building. At the counter we produced our slips of paper and driver's licenses, and gave the ticket lady a brazen stare. She asked if we were students in China. We said "Taipai." After inspecting our licenses, she gave us local prices. From Xian to Turpan in the northwest province is 36 yuan for a hard seat and 58 for a hard berth. We bought hard berths for a total of 116.60 yuan. Later we checked the prices at the People's Hotel and found that hard berth was 110 yuan per person; we had saved $50.

I read in the *China Daily* that a turtle named Galopy in the Staten Island Zoo was undergoing his fourth treatment for cancer and being transported to Tucson, Arizona, for surgery by an eminent specialist. What a privileged turtle, unlike the many disadvantaged people and animals here.

Banks and I frittered away the rest of the day at the post office looking for another issue of *China Daily* and planning a better diet. We decided against eating any more pastries. Instead we would have apples, apricots and dates, meats, vegetables, and tea, plus some apricot brandy we bought. We sat on a bench in the shade for several hours in an uncrowded park. Banks dozed off. We revisited a teahouse and passed our favorite restaurant, which was closed, and wandered the streets looking for momo soup and cold cuts, made of green beans, bean curd, peanuts, and beef. We made our first exception to the anti-sweet rule at an ice cream shop.

SOME THOUGHTS NOW

What vision did I have during my travels forty years ago? What vision do I have now? My drawings of people capture curiosity, theirs and mine, from one moment in time.

Drawings of the Yangtze River in 1983 showed the grandeur of a bluff more than seventeen hundred feet high. A boat seemed like a fly on the water by comparison. A current photo shows that the gorge has been dwarfed by dams that dramatically raised the water level, swallowing farmland and villages in the process. Was this progress? Was it the "Realization toward Modernization" proclaimed all those years ago on a train station billboard? Who knows?

Drawings of the terracotta soldiers capture their bright and jubilant faces. The half-buried soldiers exposed to light and air in the airplane hangar that housed them emitted their individuality in facial expressions and stances. The paradox was that their expression and color faded once they were exposed. Dynasties don't rule in this world any longer, even from underground.

As I revisited the pencil drawings of Westerners and Muslims in teahouses in Turpan, China, I realized we were already blending in with cultures I philosophically opposed. In one sketch, Alvin and Ruth are shown in front, and the Turpan family and some other Westerners are behind them.

In the article "A Blended Family: Her Mother Was Neanderthal, Her Father Something Else Entirely," the *New York Times* reported that genetic analysis of bones discovered in a Siberian cave hint that the prehistoric world may have been filled with "hybrid" humans. A ninety-thousand-year-old bone fragment came from a female whose mother was Neanderthal, according to an analysis of its DNA. But her father belonged to another branch of ancient humanity known as the Denisovans.

I entered the grottos along the Silk Route in the Gobi Desert where the Peking man skull was found by a Jesuit priest. Perhaps I passed this Siberian cave where the blended family had been discovered.

What I continue to find is how connected we all are, whether it's today or ninety thousand years ago.

Ruth, Alvin, and Turpan family

UIGHUR ARBORS AND KAZAKH YURTS

Six dollars a day bought food, lodging, and transportation—what would run about $160 a day at home in San Antonio. I never thought we would save by living in China.

It had been several days since I made entries in my journal. We were at the Xian station in central China, where we would wait more than five hours for the 2:30 p.m. train, a three-day sleeper ride through the Gobi Desert to Turpan. Attendants in the VIP room were anxious to learn numbers in English. We counted one to ten together and pronounced the numbers that appeared on our tickets. Two women repeated the numbers painstakingly and burst out laughing; they rattled on in Chinese about their English pronunciation.

Outside the station boys chased butterflies and captured bees with nets. They tied live bees to strings and let them fly as far as the strings allowed. Later I saw a dead bug on the sidewalk with a string attached to his leg.

We found a teahouse and sat down to enjoy two large pots of tea. Our waitress was an older woman who swept under our chairs and brought us a large pot of hot water so we could freshen our tea at leisure. We read the *China Daily* and went back to the hotel for one more shower before the long train ride. We stocked up on bread, apples, apricot brandy, and soap.

I awoke twenty-four hours into the trip. I had slept in the third bunk, where there was room to sit up without banging my head. The air was stale, the light was right above me, and the loudspeaker was near my ear. I found some cotton swabs to block out the noise. My sleep was from real fatigue, so I didn't register the discomfort. I noticed Chinese watching me sleep, so I sat up to write. They never grew tired of watching, and there was no limit to the noise on the train, especially when the loudspeaker blared a patriotic song. Chinese in general speak loudly, and their emphatic tonal shifts jar my senses.

Later in the day I finished *Beneath the Red Banner* by Lao She, a Chinese writer killed by the Gang of Four in 1966. The book is autobiographical, about Chinese society in Beijing at the turn of the century. It's beautifully written and brutally honest.

≡

We passed high green hills like those in Afghanistan, streaming over a plateau filled with crops. Mongolian people rode small horses in the fields. That evening we had dinner with two Germans, aged eighteen and twenty, who shared their instant noodles. We also had wine and bread. We discussed German politics until a chessboard was offered to us and the German challenged a Han Chinese to a game.

≡

It was July 4, but U.S. Independence Day seemed like a foreign concept as we strolled the streets of Turpan amid donkey carts, bicycles, and vegetable trucks. Down a dusty alleyway and into an immense inner courtyard we found a marketplace filled with Uighurs, the ethnic borderland Chinese who are partially Eastern European, partially Mongolian. Many had blue or hazel eyes. They sold striped watermelons, grapes, pita bread, meat dumplings and rice, green peppers, mutton chops, live goats and donkeys, and an odd assortment of clothing. The dumplings caught my attention, so we stopped in a covered pavilion to satiate our growling stomachs. I couldn't remember my stomach ever growling back home. Curry seasoning widened our nostrils and enhanced our appetites with its intoxicating smell. Mildly flavored tea and dumplings filled us for one yuan each (fifty cents). We then bargained for a striped watermelon with a rind so sweet that the Uighurs ate it.

Chinese in agricultural fields

On the main street we bargained for a donkey cart to take us to the Jiaohe ruins, once a prominent city along the Silk Road. For five yuan we found a medium-sized, fairly fat donkey that I felt could pull four people comfortably for ten miles. We bumped through tree-lined back roads that soon became dirt tracks. Crossing irrigation channels and dodging potholes, I realized what a good donkey we had.

This donkey showed a singular interest, as his ears perked up at any view of another donkey within a hundred feet. He let out a long bray when his nostrils filled with the scent of another male so close. He farted as he exerted his call, and his pace quickened. The driver slapped an elm twig across his back side. Clip, clop created our rhythm and music as the donkey

Peace Park, China

jingled his tack chains. The miniature saddle kept sliding to one side, but the driver used a stick to straighten it. Perhaps it was for children to ride later. The donkey lowered his head to sniff each turd in the path. He took his time, though whacks

Turpan

fell on him repeatedly. Wheat was spread out in the middle of the road so the weight of the carts and trucks could separate it from the chaff. The donkey took a large bite of wheat, never altering his pace. He slowed to enter a shallow stream as he couldn't judge its depths. He paused midstream to piss. His narrow hooves etched into the road winding up the hill as he pulled with the majority of his strength. I hopped off to lessen the load. On descending the hill, the donkey braced himself on the front of the cart and leaned back on his haunches to break the momentum. He started to slip and became unstable and he guided the cart toward the bank to stop. Banks jumped out of the small flatbed to lighten the load, and the driver allowed the animal to set his own stride. Amazing beast, although often thought of as ordinary.

I listed all of the ethnic groups and religions in my journal. I never knew how diverse China was, with Korean, Turkish, Tibetan, Arabian, and Mongolian intermarriages with the Han.

One morning on our usual stroll, a Uighur motioned us into his home. It felt subversive for some reason, but he was friendly once we were inside and spoke good English, as did his family. Chen Pu Tsung's wife fixed us six courses of a nutritional meal with bean curd soup, rice, and watermelon to complete it. The sardines, green peppers, and green beans with beef, eggs, tomatoes were all so tasty. We drank sparkling soda and talked for several hours. Chen turned out to be a professor who taught geography at Xinjiang University. His wife taught at August 1 Military Middle School, which had two thousand students. His son spoke Russian and taught Chinese. His daughter taught geography and studied Chinese art. Both children lived in the family's two-bedroom home, which shared a courtyard with the middle school.

Chen described his classmates of 1949 from Hangzhou University. One, a millionaire in Los Angeles, had built the famed Fung Lum restaurant on the grounds of Universal Studios. The Pang family invested $5 million to construct the restaurant to look like the Tang dynasty temple. Another classmate taught Chinese history at Brown University and the University of Pittsburgh. Another classmate was still in China at the Academy of Sciences.

We were so grateful for the generosity and invited Chen and his family to Texas for some "yee-haw" hospitality, though we all knew we would probably never see each other again.

The Xinjiang Uighur Autonomous Region spanned vast deserts, lakes, and mountains in the northwestern part of China. The Uighurs were so open and friendly toward travelers. In Turpan most families let their young children run out

Muslim in turret

from their clay open-air homes to wave and say goodbye. In cafés men invited us to join them in drinking cognac any time of day. They seemed to be devoted Muslims but still enjoyed drinking and talking to me, even though men normally don't speak to women in public.

Walking back through an oasis-irrigated wheat and melon field, we came upon a small clay village. A family waved us over to sit under a mature grape arbor to eat green grapes and sip tea. I spent the rest of the day sketching portraits of the family, whose members lined up to be drawn. The women prepared noodles as the men sat with us. We did not have a language in common, but we felt comfortable this way. Banks and

I sang "Yesterday," "Give Peace a Chance," and other Beatles songs to liven the group. Then they began singing folk songs. We ate together, and I gave them extra drawings of the grandmother, three sons, and a daughter-in-law and grandson. I had tried to capture their dignified manner, colorful dress, and high cheekbones. Cultures could unite through the arts as our common language.

The Uighurs' Indo-European language sounded like a blend of English, Mongolian, and Turkish. Women wore knee-length large floral print dresses and opaque, ochre-colored thigh-high hose, striped elastic garter belts, and multicolored bloomers tucked into their hose. Money was kept in the knees, creating impressive bulges. Their hair was tucked under transparent, shimmering scarves, with long dark braids resting on their backs. Men had shaved heads and wore stiff, round Muslim prayer caps.

This village was a small maze of high red clay walls leading to inner courtyards of grapevine arbors and open-air kitchens. The Gobi Desert baked red clay bricks without much effort.

Donkeys pulled up to ten times their weight, lugging flatbed carts slightly narrower than double beds. They took us to desert ruins and the grottos where Pierre Teilhard de Chardin discovered the Peking Man skull in the 1930s. How differently the Uighurs lived compared to the mainland Han Chinese. There was greater expression and freedom in these border ethnic groups. It was a refreshing change from life among the Hans.

Neither the Kazakhs nor the Uighurs liked the rule of the Hans. I saw five to seven children per family here in the small villages. The Han communist government couldn't regulate the policy of one child per family so far from Beijing, which was a three-day coal train ride across the top of China from Turpan. We were in the farthest northwest area travelers were permitted to see. The border town of Kashgar even farther west was closed to travelers in 1981 when riots broke out between minorities and the Hans.

Six weeks in China had given us ample time to reflect on the Han daily routines in most of the country. Although Hans had an enriched, ancient cultural history, they seemed to live a nonchallenging, drab existence. After visiting at least fifteen major cities, I noted that many elders employed themselves selling popsicles on the streets from padded wooden boxes made from old baby carriages. Seven to ten often gathered in one spot outside a movie theater or school to sell these treats at five fin (two and a half cents) apiece. I appreciated class struggles to make a better living, but the Han government allowed no freedom and had little respect for human rights. I would take living in border regions like Turpan any day to living in crowded major cities where there was little ambition or incentive. The average person, rural or suburban, was yoked to a government that robbed them of the fruits of their labor.

I was in a desert yet lacked nothing. I felt at home with a people I had never seen before and a language I had never heard, embraced by the Uighurs as one caring family. Within this desert plain the oasis cities sprang up. I was leaving a fertile culture. The people here showed such dignity, grace, hospitality, and love for differences as they lived in peace.

On our three-day train ride out of the Gobi Desert through Inner Mongolia to Beijing, we passed miles of rocky wasteland as the Tian Shan Mountains faded from us on the distant horizon. I always got depressed as I felt the land flattening out. A docile dragon tail.

Our train chugged past where the Great Wall ended in Jiuquan at the western edge of the desert. The wall was dilapidated, the end of a defeated dragon's tail.

☰

Turpan family making noodles

Turpan son

Turpan grandfather

Turpan grandson

When Banks and I arrived in Hong Kong to enter China, there wasn't even a current *Lonely Planet* guide. China was in flux. Only by word of mouth did we learn how to navigate what turned out to be three months of wandering indiscriminately through a vast, complex Eastern culture.

We traveled unofficially during a window of opportunity for Westerners when China was just opening to democracy. We were blessed not to be classified as an English teacher and spouse and were guided by people in Hong Kong who knew the system, which was to start with the only permit available—a three-week visa. The more rural and farther from Beijing we got, the more likely we could extend our visas another month, then another month. Who could have known?

≡

Humans still aren't valued as having any basic rights by China's military regime. The government is taking away any freedoms gained simply because they can. Humans belong to the government for use as it sees fit. Hong Kong is in riots over trying to be one country in China with two states. How did we ever accept that this would work, given the Chinese feudal history?

In China we learned how to judge information. If those we encountered seemed honest and authentic, we trusted their information. There were no cell phones or internet.

We had total freedom to meet Chinese in their homes. We didn't need to communicate in a common language but shared through the arts: music, drawing, cuisine, love and respect for our particular identities.

What if, instead of just doing pilgrimages to holy places, a natural movement evolved in which people purposefully lived, if only briefly, in foreign cultures to share their customs through culinary, visual, and performance arts as the common language?

There's an urgency in our wirelessly connected world today to be aware of the Uighur and Kazakh plight. The Uighur culture was thriving in 1983, but where is it now? Will these cultures I've grown to feel compassion for ultimately be rediscovered as broken bones and terracotta remnants?

≡

We finally boarded a coal train for the fourteen-hour ride to Lake Tianchi in the mountains of northwestern China, though my heart splintered thinking of leaving that family in Turpan.

The Kazakhs in this ethnic region lived in yurts and seemed very hospitable. Four chess games later the German, a second-division champion in Hamburg, was still beating the Chinese.

Coal specks coated my arm, which rested in the open window; the dusting made me look like a dalmatian. Teacups banged under scalding water as attendants poured tea for people in hard berths. With a low whistle, the wheels below began to roll after a short station delay. The baggage was in rows above the windows; the people were in rows on the beds and seats below.

≡

We were still on the train, and I woke several times in the early morning light, which cast the desert and mountains in deep blues. I rearranged the sheet and blanket over my shoulders. I thought Banks was caressing my back but woke to find a Chinese tucking in my blanket so it wouldn't touch the floor. I slept lightly for another hour. Chinese generally rose early and talked over morning noodles; these particular Chinese were proud to be eating instant noodles. They were from Hong Kong, where they didn't eat Chinese food all the time and lorded it over inhabitants of China who could never visit their liberated city. I was glad I awoke before the loudspeaker began blaring the top ten Chinese tunes. I knew them well, having heard them over and over the past thirty-six hours. "Do-Re-Mi" from *The Sound of Music* was particularly popular.

☰

We finally arrived and found ourselves enthralled by a lake that Swiss travelers say reminds them of home. Lake Tianchi, in Ürümqi, was in the farthest northwestern region of China. Its clear, placid stretch of several miles carved through a verdant valley and pine forest. Mountains were tipped by glaciers. Morning light warmed the lime-green clover fields, scattered with fat-tailed sheep and long-eared goats.

We spent a week relaxing in a yurt overlooking Lake Tianchi. Visitors that walked through the yurt's four-foot door included three angora goats at once and two kid goats that had the dignity to come in one at a time. The goats immediately began nibbling the wooden lattice structure, while the kids nonchalantly gave a lick or nuzzled the china bowl or woolen carpet. I had never thought of them as house pets, but I was keeping my mind open.

Glacial peaks rose more than sixteen thousand feet above the lake and fed swift chilling streams that emptied into it. Extreme contours dipped down to the valley until the mountains lessened. Cattle, sheep, and goats scattered across the clover fields while Kazakhs riding small Mongolian ponies attempted to group them and move them to higher pastures. Wildflowers brightened the luscious landscape with blues, purples, yellows, and whites. Cows ripped the tender shoots in a hunger-crazed manner, as if their plump bellies were hollow.

Lake Tianchi in the Kazakh mountains

A crisp summer breeze refreshed the sunlit portion of my body and chilled the rest.

A Kazakh rode by me, his straight torso towering above his pony. He had draped precious sika antlers across the brass saddle horn. Mountain Kazakhs generally wore knee-high black leather boots, black corduroy pants that bagged around their waist, thick woven cotton shirts, black woolen vests, and white Turkish turbans. I found the land and people here extraordinary in the way they lived on their own terms.

We traveled on foot to visit one yurt after another and were welcomed generously. Every yurt consisted of a muffin-shaped tent with lattice wooden poles that reached toward the center top, leaving a hole two feet in diameter for ventilation. The

Kazakh yurts around Lake Tianchi

outside was covered by thick canvas blankets and a four-foot-high wooden door. A wooden platform covered the interior area, except for a rectangular space leading from the door to the center so a person could enter without taking off his or her shoes. Beautiful Uighur and Kazakh woolen carpet designs brightened the rooms like wildflowers in a clover field. For real warmth at night we sank into thick satin quilts filled with top-quality wool. Five people fit comfortably, but often up to eleven slept in one yurt.

Another Kazakh passed by, riding a steer with the simplest wooden tree saddle and no bridle. A woman followed close behind as they wound their way uphill.

Kazakh Muslim family near Lake Tianchi

We rented one yurt for two yuan a person, which included a large thermos of hot water for tea, small china bowls used as teacups, and a basin of lukewarm water for washing. Meals cost between 1 and 1.50 yuan for fresh mutton and green beans over rice, tender liver and onions over rice, or green vegetables over rice. In the mornings a Kazakh milked a cow for delicious hot milk, thirty fin a cup. This milk, when diluted, had the consistency of cottage cheese without the curdled texture.

On our southern side were the Qilian Shan Mountains, on the other the Alashan Desert. Bleached bones were scattered among rounded stones along dirt ridges. The land turned green with lush crops, and canals channeled oasis water to the fields. Fine-grained sand turned it back to the underlying brown. Snowcapped peaks more than thirteen thousand feet high shone in the distance.

Dromedaries' tan humps complemented the rolling countryside. I gazed out the train window to find peasants gazing in. I didn't want to head to Beijing, a three-day journey across the top of China. The beauty was here, around the lake. We seemed to yearn for an understanding our worlds forbade. The mountainside was dappled with the mauve shadows of clouds. These mimicked our steam engine's smoke-puff shadows on the sand ridges, which converged on us until we, too, seemed to be passing through clouds. Peasants built stone walls along the track or dug rows for crops.

Women's scarves protected them from the wind, which bent the trees along stone-laid canals. For peasants, the sight of us was a break from labor. Chicks chirped beneath my berth as if it were daylight, though they'd been boxed in darkness for more than thirty-six hours. Patches of weed flourished along cracked gullies. Squares and circles in a dried moat reminded me of Neolithic cultures once formidable on the earth.

Wheat and maize crops rose two or three feet, bordered by elm and poplar. Mesozoic and Paleozoic rocks streamed by in red and brown ribbons. A Muslim Chinese offered us a hardboiled egg. He said his ancestors were from Arabia or Iran. The Chinese three bunks down drank wine and played a finger-betting game, guessing what numbers would show up. We finished our apples and brandy and thought about leaving China. It was time, though we didn't know where we'd go, beyond possibly taking the Trans-Siberian Railway from Beijing to Moscow.

☰

Banks napping on the Great Wall near Beijing

At the Kunlun in Ürümqi, the official guest hotel, we waited four days for train tickets to Beijing that we could only book through the hotel. We paid two hundred yuan each for hard sleepers for the three days across the top of China. Each day we asked the management for our tickets, and each day we were told to come back the next day. We finally asked for a refund, never got it, and decided we could get the tickets at the train station. No Chinese in the hotel took responsibility or answered any questions. It seemed they were afraid to deal with foreigners for fear of being punished.

At this hotel the women and men were separated, and I met two college-aged women who taught English and were returning to London and New York. We had four beds to a room for three yuan a night. The English woman said she had been kicked out of the isolated university near Shanghai seven months into her twelve-month contract. No reasons were given except that the administration didn't like her attitude about petty rules and regulations. They saw her students start to question authority, refuse to sign in on the register, and even burn the sections of the sign-in sheet. The woman from New York was working through Cornell University and taught in Chengdu. She felt that this city was more open to Westerners, even playing baseball with students. She had studied Mandarin for two years before arriving and expected to have a teacher for her own studies as well, but none became available even though it was in the contract.

These women left, and I shared a room with a Hong Kong Chinese and a mainland Chinese. Both were friendly but wouldn't speak English.

☰

SOME THOUGHTS NOW

The Great Wall is still dilapidated when you leave Beijing and travel west. It's crumbled; the mighty dragon abandoned its shell long ago.

China still uses coal trains as the world adjusts to renewable technologies. But its government has surpassed the rest of the world in its use of surveillance technology. Cameras are everywhere to track each thought and movement of people on the street. They will arrest someone with ethnic bone structure walking home, based on facial recognition. Is that really a crime? More than three million people in internment camps are paying the price.

Can you imagine being free to wander from yurt to yurt in the Kazakh Mountains to celebrate Ramadan today? I never understood, in the 1980s, that an intimate sharing between foreigners there might never be possible again.

The Kazakhs, like the Uighurs, are being detained in "re-education" camps. Kazakhstan borders China and has more of a balance of power, appeasing Beijing while defending its own citizens interned in Xinjiang. Most recently the Black Chinese in Guangzhou are also being persecuted.

The world may soon no longer know the Uighur, Kazakh, Tibetan, and other ethnic customs that we once shared through the common language of faith, cuisine, art, and respect for human life.

RAILS OF TRANS-SIBERIA

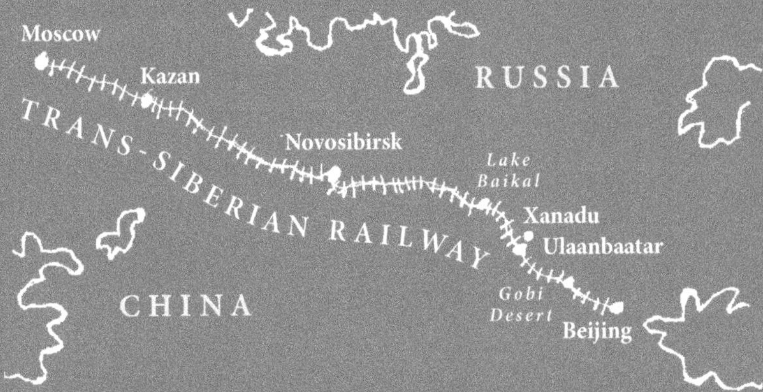

Chinese ticket for Trans-Siberian Railway

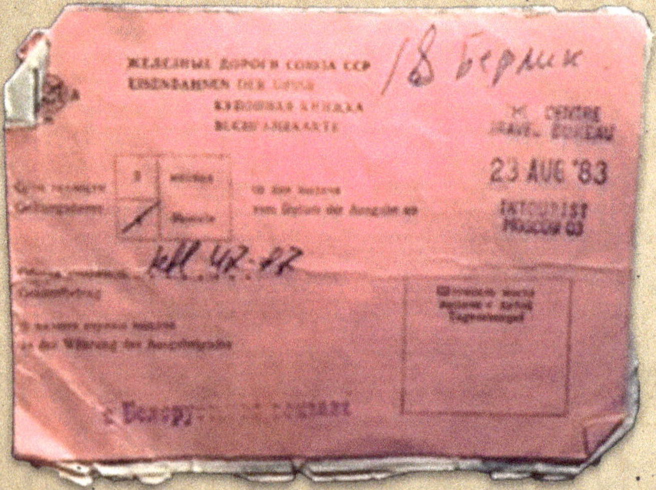

Form for entry to Moscow

BEIJING TO MOSCOW

A Swedish groom studying a year in Beijing and his Chinese bride took unoccupied beds on the left. They were heading for Sweden as she broke permanently from her tradition.

三

The Trans-Siberian Railway flew through the Inner Mongolian grasslands as we traveled the six days from Beijing to Moscow. Dryish green prairies of foot-high grass stretched for miles. Alluvial sands held the roots loosely, and herds of short-horned cattle and fat-tailed sheep cropped the roots from the sand, imprinting it with their hooves and mouths. The land sprang back once the herds passed. Panicked sheep veered to the right of the train in a perfect arch. Herds of Mongolian horses broke the flat horizon with their rounded ceramic forms. A cerulean sky approximated their curves to muffin-shaped yurts. Square mud huts popped up like shooting targets in a row and dropped back into the sand.

Our compartment had four beds with cushion pillows, wool blankets, and white starched sheets draped over them. A thick oriental carpet in plum, navy, steel blue, and tan covered the floor and long hallway, leading to nine similar compartments. A wide glass window with parted curtains invited me to glimpse what felt like an untouchable world. Luxury absorbed me as I sank down in the cushions. The tiny oscillating fan and reading lights over each bed didn't turn off arbitrarily, as happened on Chinese trains. Broad windows across the hall and over our table set off apples and pears against a white tablecloth and blue and white teacups.

A Swedish groom studying for a year in Shanghai and his Chinese bride took the unoccupied beds on the left. They were heading for Sweden as she broke permanently from her tradition. How painful to make such a decision so young in life.

Crossing the border from China to the Soviet Union, we were detained for two hours while the train wheels were switched. Mongolian tracks were wider than Chinese tracks, so each coach was lifted by cable and pushed away, with new wheels lowered onto the tracks and rolled under the coaches. Banks and I walked through the train station, which was lit with Christmas bulbs, and were ushered back to the train by a police officer when curiosity took us out a back door.

Once we were in our compartment, our passports were returned stamped with our exit visas from China. After an hour on the new tracks we halted; two police officers clicked their heels together at our doorway and took our passports again. They were returned just before we reached Moscow. That afternoon in the dining car we saw Evans Revere, whom we had talked with at the Russian embassy in Beijing, although he worked at the American embassy. He was traveling with his wife and ten- and two-year-old daughters in a coach above first class. After sharing a meal of spicy green peppers with pork we walked two coaches up to a rosewood room filled with brass ashtrays and door handles, green velvet curtains, plush couches, and chairs. A washbasin connected the living room to the bedroom. We discussed the Korean War briefly, since Revere's wife was Korean and he had lived in Seoul.

Ξ

It was 1 a.m. and the train rolled through a silent town. Each blocky house looked alike—floodlit dark windows amid

Aspens in Siberia

emptiness. The quarter moon dimmed behind clouds. Stars vanished. I was lulled back to sleep.

We stopped around 9 a.m. at a town that was not on our Chinese map. Several tourists took the platform steps toward the town and were turned back by Mongolian police, who then motioned for any Mongols hanging around the station doors to go back inside. They peered out at us through square panes. Goats wandered onto the platform, having more freedom than humans.

Our Swedish roommate and his wife sang the popular Chinese songs played over the loudspeaker.

I caught a glimpse of a dapple-gray pony standing by his master, who wore a white turban, a green and white skirt to his knees, white tapered pants, and black knee-high riding boots.

Three hawks chased each other, then four. White heads, brown and white speckled bodies, black wingtips, and white fan-tails. A marmot snooped around a fencepost and darted down a hole. A lone horseman on the wide-open plains emerged from a smudge on the horizon.

Ξ

Our coach was the twelfth car of thirteen, which meant a walk through four cars to the dining car in front. We now had a Mongolian diner serving mutton chops. The first day there was plenty of food. The next two days we ordered what was

View from train window

available, usually pumpernickel bread and butter. We always paid in U.S. dollars and took change in Mongolian currency at a rate of 3.3 to 1. We exchanged money with a Westerner and bought two loaves of bread, sausage, and cucumbers. The cucumbers were as succulent as watermelons.

The third day of our journey we stopped for twenty minutes at Ulaanbaatar and walked around the station platform. The Russian men were stocky, with imposing noses and ruddy faces. Mongols wore white smocks that hit right below the knee. A colored sash offset the white and the black knee-high boots.

Small frame houses with brightly painted gingerbread fronts dotted the landscape. Picket fences framed yards. These homes looked like the logging villages around Ketchikan or Wrangell, Alaska, in the Inland Passage.

Homing pigeons kept pace with our coach. Two Mongolian horsemen galloped up to the tracks, keeping pace with the train for several hundred yards and waving their bowler-style hats. Their ponies slowed, and they waved a last time and turned toward the fields.

SOME THOUGHTS NOW

I'll probably never sit on a Chinese-Russian train for six days again, reading *Crime and Punishment* and rolling through Mongolian grasslands, Siberian forests, and Ural Mountain lakes. I treasure that time and those memories.

What still rolls through my head is the world's extraordinary potential to live in harmony. Even the sausage, sauerkraut, and beer shortage in the Russian diner car added to the train during those last three days is an amusement rather than a worry, although I did stock up on beer. I thought more about why I did as I pondered Dostoevsky's life, his experience being in a multiethnic and multidenominational noble family, and his mental anguish, the moral dilemmas that played out in *Crime and Punishment*. The protagonist, Raskolnikov, formulates a plan to kill an unscrupulous pawnbroker for her money. Before the killing, he thinks that with that money he could liberate himself from poverty and perform great deeds, but confusion and hesitation foil his plan for a morally justifiable killing. Dostoevsky was timely and is still relevant in asking the global question of whether greed can ever morally justify hoarding and killing.

As my 1980s travels percolated, my questions deepened. At first I just walked through Hindu living rooms that were actually the dense streets of Calcutta. I stared into Mother Teresa's still, dark eyes, an Albanian in an Indian culture, as she handed me a baby in her orphanage. She spoke the common language of compassion for human suffering, which was just germinating in me. She recognized that no one needed to suffer at the hands of another because of greed, religious differences, racial tensions, political alliances, or corruption and even took money from criminals to feed the poor. Through their writing and actions, Dostoevsky and Mother Teresa transformed not only the world but also my own heart.

I recently spent the night in my own church, Saint John's Episcopal in New Braunfels, Texas. Our church sisters housed three mothers and children who were looking for homes and jobs. The Family Promise program allows people to spend weeks in different churches as safe places. I brought modeling clay for the kids. One mother was deaf and had just come from Mississippi with her four children. The oldest was in sixth grade, and the youngest was five months old. I'd never seen such a tight-knit family, with the hearing children communicating to the mother and she to them through signing. I was touched by their desire to better themselves. As I bottle-fed the five-month-old, I thought again of that orphaned Indian baby I'd held in Calcutta. I felt a palpable love for humanity. This is the wishbone I now understand, where we all have long or short splits but it's the same bone.

HOARD THE BEER

Mao reportedly once instituted a policy that every Han must kill ten flies a day to eradicate an overabundance. These two Han remained loyal swatters, walking the passageway and whacking flies.

We were on the Soviet-Mongolian border passing through Soviet customs. A Mongolian checked our passports as the train started to roll again. He was looking for an Italian who was later found visiting a friend. The official seemed distracted as we headed into the Soviet Union, and the train engineer was asked to stop on this side of the border just long enough for him to jump off. He shook hands with the ground attendant, looking relieved.

Rounding a bend, we saw streetlights, and the train came to a stop. We had just passed through a heavy wire fence and were officially in the Soviet Union. About twenty police officers waited to board the train. Three swiftly came into our compartment and began searching the ceiling and floor. We were asked for our passports and told to wait outside the compartment. The officers clearly didn't trust us, and we didn't trust them. We were handed declaration forms for cameras and money and told to exchange money at a nearby building—cash only, U.S. dollars, no traveler's checks, seventy-six cents to $1. We knew we could get five times this on the streets of

Moscow. It was 8:30 p.m. Moscow time and 1:30 a.m. Beijing time. The orange quarter moon vanished behind the clouds.

≡

The young officials had flushed faces, serious expressions, and a formal manner. Shifts in their gazes told me they were practicing what they'd been trained to do but weren't brainwashed by it.

A Soviet dining car appeared along with Soviet sleeping cars. The grapevine predicted a shortage of food from here on in.

A huge white moth landed outside my window, beat its wings against the pane, and dropped from sight. What kind of omen was this? I was still reading *Crime and Punishment.* Raskolnikov had just murdered his landlady and her sister. I saw four white moths clinging to a streetlight.

Four days into the journey I awoke to a crystal-clear lake the size of Tennessee. If it were in the United States, there would have been campers on the shoreline. Here there was nothing but unspoiled beauty. We had been following the lake's southwestern edge for forty-five minutes. Birch trees lined the shore, and logging posts were scattered at the edge. The crisp, cool air was invigorating, and I was overwhelmed by the vast amount of underutilized natural resources. Conical haystacks built around slender birch trunks dotted the small wheat fields.

Banks and I walked four cars to the Russian diner, pretending a new restaurant had just opened in our neighborhood. Two women waited on us without smile or question. Bread, sausage, olive and onion soup, and hot cocoa were the most appetizing offerings.

≡

Train depot in Outer Mongolia

The train pulled into a small village somewhere in Outer Mongolia. Women filled the platform selling hot potatoes, carrots, green beans, raspberries, and blueberries. We bought two cups of raspberries for fifty kopeks each and ate them on the spot. Gypsy girls paraded in colorful skirts and flowing hair, asking for vodka, money, and attention from the wealthier tourists. Several boys asked if I was from the United States. They glowed with pride at communicating. One said he had a T-shirt with the mountains of Oregon on it. A train coming our way made us jump across the tracks to our own side. We waved goodbye.

The only Chinese we saw were two Han diplomats from Hungary. They kept to their compartments and only ventured to the passage window when the train stopped. They seemed timid outside their own country.

Mao reportedly once instituted a policy that every Han must kill ten flies a day to eradicate an overabundance. These two Han remained loyal swatters, walking the passageway and whacking flies. On occasion they even ducked into rooms to bag one. Apparently not every Han had done their part, because there was still plenty of buzzing. Banks crippled a fly in our room and dropped it on the carpet outside the door. In no time the diplomatic Han was there to bring down a swatter on the one-legged buzzing dipterid. Victory.

☰

SOME THOUGHTS NOW

Maury Maverick, a crusty San Antonio icon, published articles from time to time in the *San Antonio Express-News* about our journey. He depicted us as illustrious young visionaries, much to our surprise. When we returned from our travels Banks was courted by the top law firms in town and could be particular about terms because we were portrayed as engaging and smart and had dodged the major real estate bust in Texas. We didn't have children yet and had chosen to travel in Asia while we were young and unencumbered by debt.

I returned to my roots in Alamo Heights in 1984. I was freshly digesting our odyssey and didn't yet know what it meant or what effect, if any, it had on me. Building on my work as an English teacher, artist, and writer, I obtained a doctorate in English literature from England, continued to paint watercolor portraits of houses for my San Antonio friends, and wrote.

One of my first watercolors upon returning was commissioned by a friend, congressman Lamar Smith. Other friends

Bexar County Courthouse, San Antonio, Texas

asked me to paint watercolors of their homes on site. I thought perhaps this might become my career. My 1984 painting of the Bexar County Courthouse is still displayed between two flags behind Lamar's desk in his San Antonio office.

≡

Life was unexpected and rich when I kept my mind open to exploration. I was asked to teach beginning Spanish to children ages three to six at Saint Mary's Hall Montessori School and subsequently received a Holt Foundation grant to create an integrated arts and sciences Spanish curriculum. I tweaked this as I had my first daughter, Morgan, in 1985, and my son, Wright, in 1987.

Our family traveled to many Spanish-speaking countries and rented houses for a month in the summers of 1990 and 1991 so our children could develop an appreciation for other cultures by living in them—just what I loved. We explored Antigua, Guatemala, and San Cristóbal de las Casas, and I took Spanish classes with the kids and wandered the markets and town squares. I cherished seeing the world through my young children's eyes.

Wright, Morgan, and me, San Cristóbal, Guatemala

MOSCOW TO BERLIN: *ERO LOCO*

If he was caught selling things on the streets of Moscow, he could be deported back to Zimbabwe, and the proof would likely be film of him in the act.

≡

We now had the compartment to ourselves, as the Swede and his bride were assigned a vacant room. I moved to the other lower bed. We locked the door, turned on the fan, opened the window for a crisp breeze, and undressed. We groped for softness and hardness, found them, and a train thundered by going the other direction, two feet away at a combined speed of 110 miles an hour. Windows of blurred people flashed by like a fast-forwarded Polanski movie. *Ero loco* (erotic locomotion).

≡

Sleep. Trains, trains, trains. They passed us constantly as we neared Moscow, some of them carrying military cargo heading for the Mongolian border. Rocket platforms, trucks, and jeeps—closed boxcars radiated armed might as they went by.

The five-hour time difference between Beijing and Berlin could be taken in stages so there was no jet lag. I loved asking someone what time it was. I got Beijing time, Mongolian time, local time, Moscow time. I had never experienced people using so many different time references, all keeping to their native time and translating to Moscow if need be.

Russian military vehicles

≡

The next day brought more wheat fields and wood-frame houses with picket fences. Some haystacks had roofs. A muddy white horse waited while his owner unloaded milk cans. Women bent over vegetable plots, gathering potatoes, carrots, and cabbages. Sometimes one glanced at the train.

We had a small gathering at 1:21 p.m. Moscow time at the windows in the passageway as we passed through the Ural Mountains. An obelisk marked where Asia changed to Europe. The mountains were fairly flat and heavily forested. The train ascended slowly for about twenty minutes and skated down the other side of a slope. This was the first time I had been to Europe, and what a unique way to enter. I don't know of anyone else who has come through the Urals to get to Europe!

Car no. 9 threw a small party for a dozen people celebrating the last night on the Trans-Siberian Railway. Several Oxford

Frame houses and picket fences in Siberia

students engaged in a conversation about Chinese communism. Four Poles offered me Russian beer and champagne. Sipping champagne and sitting back, I saw that most were students from prestigious universities returning to Europe after a summer of learning Mandarin. They expressed favorable yet rather superficial views of China and its people.

Another day passed, and I finished *Crime and Punishment.* A train went by, shadowing the last page until the sun peeked through for an instant between the cars. I was surprised at the book's inclination toward Christianity as a guiding force to freedom. We passed several small villages with Russian Orthodox churches still standing on waste lots. If the shells

Russian dining car

of the churches had not been destroyed, what loyalties, I wondered, lurked in the inner structure of their hearts?

We were paralleling a wide clear river. A couple played badminton along its grassy slopes while handsome German shepherds jumped for the cock.

We got a ten-minute stop. Rushing off the train, we brushed past the Chinese attendants polishing stair rails. Russian women bundled in headscarves and thick sweaters sold bright orange carrots, hot potatoes, coleslaw, tomatoes, and cucumbers. They seemed to be chuckling to themselves. Fish cakes, sausage, candy, cookies, and canned sardines crammed the kiosk windows, and a line of Europeans and Americans

Farmland in Siberia

curved around it like the Great Wall. The whistle blew. Brakes released, wheels turned. The line dissolved in all directions as we scrambled back aboard.

I had planned to sell my blue jeans for eighty rubles but wore them instead since the weather was cooler. We barreled through birch and fir with intermittent views of ample wheat fields. Haycocks and ricks were piled high amid the golden stubble. There were few inhabitants. Wooden frame houses with bright shutters had deep-sloped tin roofs that gave them an insulated look. Even in late summer I felt a chill in the air. We pulled into another station but weren't allowed to deboard. Another train was stopped, filled with Russians. They stared through windowpanes, and we stared back. Occasionally we saw a hand move or a passenger smile, but faces mostly remained blank.

Birch leaves dangled like shell chimes. Olive-colored trunks craned up toward a cloudy sky.

≡

The Chinese attendants stood erect by the doors at railway stations and seemed proud of their blue uniforms. At the same time they seemed threatened outside of China.

Telephone wires slanted up and down in smooth patterns at the top of my window as we picked up speed again. Five or six wires spread, converged on poles, spread again like people waltzing. Birch trunks shot up behind the wires.

≡

Finally, after six days, we reached Moscow with no map, no rubles, and no notion of where we'd like to head, though we would need to leave in two days. There seemed to be little time to sell my jeans and go to the Bolshoi.

The official tourist hotel cost fifty dollars a night. Coming from Asia, we thought this sounded steep. Two dollars a night was the most we had paid for clean, comfortable, popular places. We decided to sleep in the train station, not wanting to part with our U.S. dollars, the currency they'd accept.

The station was elegant, with high marble vaulting and skylights. Many ethnic groups camped in chairs for the night, and the station filled with quiet people. Banks and I spread newspapers on the floor and lay down next to a pillar. Around 2 a.m. I was awakened by a buzzing sound; it was a floor polisher running a buffer under my newspaper.

≡

Banks decided to change money on the black market. In the shadow of the Kremlin, with its high walls and spirals, two men appeared out of nowhere and made an offer, saying we could get five times the official rate. We showed them a fifty-dollar

Russian block-style housing in Beijing

bill, and they counted out the exchange from a folded wad. I thought we should recount it, but Banks felt an urge to leave. We rounded a corner. I asked him again to count it; he did and found the bills folded to be counted twice, so we only got three times the official rate. We looked around for the dealers, knowing we wouldn't see them but wanting a word or two.

I was wearing my blue jeans when a person approached with an offer. We settled on seventy rubles, but then I had to take them off. I found a restroom a block away, changed to a pair of jogging shorts from our daypack, and returned to find no one around. Soon another person approached and asked if I had stockings for sale. I said no. Everyone spoke good English, but deals were hard to make where there was paranoia.

≡

We bought tickets for a train to Berlin via Poland, and on this journey we made acquaintance with a Russian army officer and a Zimbabwean student studying surgery in Moscow. As the night wore on, we drank more vodka and the conversation flowed. The student translated for us. The Russian's wife and eight-year-old daughter stayed quiet, watchful. The daughter wore a gold cross around her neck. When I asked if they believed in practicing religions, the Russian said they were aware of them but practiced none. Soon the daughter tucked the cross under her sweater. He described shooting down American planes with cannon in Vietnam. We moved on to freedom of speech. Banks said if we wanted to say Reagan was a son of a bitch we easily could, but it was harder to say that of Gorbachev. Here the conversation disintegrated, and we went to bed.

The next day a student who befriended us told us what it was like to study in Moscow. He'd been there for three years and had three to go. A full scholarship gave him a modest place to stay and board. There was no allowance for clothes or personal items, so he bought and sold on the black market. Crossing the Russian-Polish border, he had hidden ten $100 bills around the room so officials wouldn't confiscate them. One was crinkled up between two layers of aluminum foil that had been wrapped around roast chicken; others were in window frames and the lining of luggage. He bought Western goods in Berlin—albums, hosiery, dresses—to sell in Moscow, returning to Berlin every three or four months to restock. If he was caught selling things on the streets of Moscow, he could be deported back to Zimbabwe, and the proof would likely be film of him in the act. The officials would call him up and ask if he wanted to see himself star in a movie.

We got to Berlin at 11 p.m., with no deutsche marks and no place to stay. The student took us to a bed-and-breakfast. On the way he bought a loaf of white bread to go with his hundred-dollar roasted chicken. We checked in and snacked on his favorites, all of us famished. The next day we exchanged addresses, and he told us to visit his family in Zimbabwe if we could. We wished him well with his studies.

≡

SOME THOUGHTS NOW

What I so casually had then is lost. Travelers, international students, and locals used to mingle in moments that were intimate and authentic. The naivete I had, as did most Europeans we traveled with from Beijing to Moscow, vanished as quickly as it took to switch the train wheels from Chinese to Russian while we sat lifted high in the car. The trains and the same tracks are still used. My ride exists only in writing and sketches.

Now the region has "progress." Who's progressing? Who's repressed further in the process? Gentrification benefits the wealthy and is not better for every stakeholder.

The Great Wall of capitalism creeps in. I looked online at the cost to take this trip now. The train's four-bed compartment is the same size and layout but has clean flowered linens for an exorbitant price. The profit goes to a European company for the most part, so the locals lose out again in their own sacred land.

Where's the simple oscillating fan and overhead bed lights that wouldn't turn off? In that same renovation, I lost a naivete that protected me. I believed the world would embrace our differences and we would prosper together in fair trade. My part then was in living with people of other religions, cultures, and languages and accepting the local customs while I was there. I'd simply give and feel the love and then bring it home.

I went online again to explore booking the Trans-Siberian Railway. How disappointing this is—no more problem-solving or adventure of the unknown. It's like having Cliff Notes before

Kremlin drawing from a letter I wrote

reading a novel. Every detail, including many I never knew I needed, is laid out for me. Here is just a sense of it: I knew now on a computer what I'd eat before I took the journey halfway around the world. The same food I had then is displayed in luscious photos and enticing descriptions, but they're still tomatoes, cabbage, potatoes, fish, and sometimes meat with dense rye bread and butter.

I think of the international students we met who seemed to have taken risks leaving their home countries. The Swedish groom and his Chinese bride on their honeymoon in our compartment. She had left Beijing, her home, on pure faith that her life would be complete. Her tradition wouldn't allow her to be culturally accepted back in her country again. At the time I didn't think much about the fact that they wanted a room to themselves but couldn't afford it.

Now the locals in villages perform unspontaneous acts when the train arrives. There is no natural interaction, no real sharing of songs or art between cultures.

Instead of paying less than $100 for two for a six-day trip, the only choice, some forty years later, is to pay $6,000 a person for the same route and space that stretches for fifteen days. You can rent the entire train for $18,000 a person.

I traveled the Trans-Siberian in the time of Reagan. I'm afraid to travel carefree in the time of Trump. Asian cultures seemed more embracing, less divisive forty years ago. But perhaps I was just naive. Had these cultures finally embraced the good and bad of capitalism? Would I try to sell my jeans in the shadow of the Kremlin? No, I don't think I want to star in my own movie the Soviet government presents to me as they lock me up.

Back in the sand again—this time riding American quarter horses trained for cutting cows from a herd so they could be lassoed and doctored. My children were grown, so this seemed like the perfect opportunity for my second husband and me to spend more than ten years, starting in 2005, competing in cutting-horse competitions. My vision homed in on training animals so I could outperform others. I never found time for faith-based activities nor understood the meaning of contemplation or reflection. I was emotionally starved, dissatisfied with what most would think was a glorified existence.

In reflecting on the long and short bones, I realize how random it is that we end up with more or less in life, whether it's measured in genes, money, illnesses, cultural tastes, or the

Me cutting a cow from a herd

country where we are born. Ultimately we discover we all have a long end and a short end of the stick as life surprises us.

How does the short side of a broken wishbone translate into how I developed a universal love for humanity? First I had to face a personal brokenness. In 2018 my son's long-term illness spiked, causing him to fall from a sixty-foot dam. His extraordinary wife, Jessica, took charge, and Wright learned to walk with a prosthetic leg. This amazing journey makes me more compassionate for all those living with suffering. Also, amid this chaos, enduring gifts of joy, love, and charity were bestowed on us. I can see how to pass these gifts on to others, even if it is just being physically present for those in need. I'm grateful daily for the mystery of Divine Love. This is the long bone that increases the meaning of this odyssey.

The Ministry of Contemplative Action initiative, or MOCA, sprang from contemplation, creative action, reflection, and some fifty years of clarity on how and why we lift up those

Me, Catherine Lillibridge, and Dana Sommers, a.k.a. the Ministry of Contemplative Action

who have the short side of the wishbone. MOCA happened organically at an event I attended with Catherine Lillibridge and Dana Sommers. As we contemplated what could be done about human trafficking after an Alamo Area Coalition against Trafficking meeting, we wandered across the street to the oldest mission in San Antonio, Concepción, for reflection. This became our way of taking sips in working with difficult, uncomfortable issues in our world. If we contemplated, acted, then reflected as a ministry we found that could be more effective, regardless of the issue. The current one is the separation of children from families at the Texas border.

It's like the biblical metaphor of living water. Giving compassion is the same as drawing water from a well and letting it live in others by passing it on to those who are thirsty. As we

Pecos River, Texas

live in other people's worlds for a while, we can see the greatest needs.

My 1980s travels still feed me daily, like living water, as I touch again those who touched me. I give to the neediest out of knowledge, spiritual passion, and adaptive perception to meet needs where I see them. In my twenties I wanted it all and had imagination but no vision or maturity. I wasn't rebellious in my own culture, just passionate about enlarging it and embracing the world.

Now I have vision and maturity to look at the wonder of life, not only with physical sight but with the "eyes of the heart." I see that my calling was germinating through expanding my horizon in Rio de Janeiro, Brazil, in 1978, or 1980s travels in Asia, or recent travels to Honduras.

Living water spews from limestone ledges in central and West Texas. Pictographs still narrate the nomadic Comanche people's story along canyon walls on Edmund James's Cedar Creek Ranch. Edmund, a longtime friend, still lives here in spirit. As we seek out the rock art and continue to appreciate ages gone by through the visual arts, our common language becomes appreciation of our humanity. MOCA, the contemplation, action of seeing and embracing diversity, and then reflection, brings universal harmony.

Traveling in Asia also changed the way I relate to animals. After ten days of camel intimacy in the Thar Desert, I will never go near a camel again.

I used to think it was cruel to see horses, camels, goats, cats, dogs, and monkeys as beasts of burden or sustenance on a dinner plate. Indian children laughed as I attempted to pet a tethered goat. Then I met a tethered monkey. His beady, fearful eyes showed me his fate wasn't to be petted but rather slaughtered. I don't desire to eat meat anymore (another aberration in Texas). I've owned horses that would only be beasts of burden in India. I still feel attached to them, but my energy has shifted to helping people in need.

I continue to kill scorpions and fleas and, well, bugs in general. I'm mindful that from the Hindu perspective I'm transgressing. I still envision a Hindu friend who had a string hanging from the ceiling where hundreds of flies perched. He would put a large bag up around the thin string and close it at the top. Flies slid off the string and into the bag, and he opened the front door and let them go. They quickly returned.

I left my own country and followed a quest for wonder, only to find the growing mystery of our universal one together. I roamed across territories, societies, and cultures without knowing Farsi, Hindi, Urdu, Mandarin, or Russian. A more prominent language emerged of discerning human trust in sharing and caring.

I'll never forget the hand that motioned me under a grapevine arbor where five generations of a Uighur family lived in the Gobi Desert. Who were they? What nationality? Several had blue or hazel eyes. They didn't know me but offered me room at the table. I sat cross-legged on a Persian rug, pulled out colored pencils and paper, and did portraits of grandparents, parents, two brothers, and four sisters. I gave them some of the originals as the women prepared a feast of noodles and fresh watermelon. Why was I so comfortable here? I was treated like family—a family sharing their humanity through the tradition of welcoming strangers.

I had tasted this agape love that brought us to a place of constant discovery of a new way to share.

ACKNOWLEDGMENTS

I'm indebted to you, the readers who open this book, and to the families in *Wishbone*, including my own and extended ones, who have shown me the way to "be" family.

I am thankful for the support of many friends, acquaintances, colleagues, and scholars. Trinity University has given gracious support through Mike Bacon, vice president for alumni relations and developement at Trinity, and an avid reader of Silk Road travel; Kyle Gillette, associate provost at the university; Lisa Endreson, manager of the university's Michael and Noémi Neidorff Art Gallery; Katsuo Nishikawa Chavez, director of Trinity's Center for International Engagement; Camille Casey and Kay Casey, former vice president of alumni relations and development at Trinity, who are friends and originators of this project; Danny Anderson, former president of Trinity; Vanessa Beasley, president of Trinity; and Erin Baker and Herb Stumberg, who are on Trinity's Board of Trustees.

Dudley Harris, an opthalmologist, potter, and friend, always photographed my children as they grew up and captured my *Wishbone* art and artifacts. Tom Payton at Trinity University Press, Kathleen Niendorff, and Joe and Diane Bigley have taken the book out of my head and onto the page.

San Antonio mayor Ron Nirenberg has been a generous supporter, as have John Casey and World Affairs Council CEO Armen Babajanian.

The Rev. Ripp Hardaway at Saint John's Episcopal Church in New Braunfels and my church family of women, spearheaded by Noreen Hendley, molded this book out of a block of clay. Lark and Erica Mason, Lark III, and Kurt Feick and Linda Ridgeway-Gaulter couldn't host my book on *Antiques Roadshow* but are my avid supporters.

Nancy Folbre, Terry McDonald, and Chuck Stark are relatives who have always supported my endeavors.

Thanks to the late Joe Russell, friend of forty years, who kept my journals, art, and artifacts in his garage for ten years when I was thinking I should throw it all away. Thanks, also, to Carol Russell, a friend.

Thanks to Banks Smith and his wife, Stephanie. Banks partnered with me on this journey and helped to create our beautiful family. He recently wrote to me: "Carol and I traveled for a year and a half in Asia as a married couple. Purposely and without a preplanned itinerary, we were free to follow the many adventures we met along the way. Carol thrived. Through courage, creativity, and endurance, she gained a unique insight into the cultures and people of Asia, and into herself." I deeply appreciate his kind words and ongoing support.

Thanks to Jim Folbre Jr., my late husband, who traveled with me through thick and thin. Thanks to my late mother, a teacher, horse enthusiast, artist, and nature lover.

Thanks to my son, Wright, and his wife, Jessica; my daughter, Morgan, and her husband, Travis; and my grandchildren, Callum and Lila, to whom this book is dedicated as they bring back my gusto for life.

Most of all, my deepest thanks to Naomi Shihab Nye, a longtime friend, fellow teacher, kindred spirit, Trinity alumna, and poet who has traveled similar roads by camel in India. Michael, Madison, Naomi and their grandson, Connor, are always family to me as we journey through love and loss.

Carol Wright Folbre is a San Antonio native living in the Texas Hill Country with more than twenty years of experience as an educator, writer, and artist.